LIFE IN EIGHT STAGES

WHAT TO KNOW TO RAISE AND BE A HUMAN

DAVID MARTINO, PH.D.

KNOWMORE PRESS

Life In Eight Stages: What to Know to Raise and Be a Human

Published by KNOWMORE PRESS
Fort Collins, CO

ISBN: 979-8-9925472-0-7 (paperback)
ISBN: 979-8-9925472-1-4 (hardcover)

PSYCHOLOGY / Developmental / Lifespan Development
FAMILY & RELATIONSHIPS / Life Stages / General

Cover deisgn by Amanda Miller, copyright owned by David Martino, Ph.D.
Interior design by Bryan Canter, copyright owned by David Martino, Ph.D.

QUANTITY PURCHASES: Schools, companies, professional groups, clubs, and other organizations may qualify for special terms when ordering quantities of this title. For information, email dr.martino2020@gmail.com.

CONTENTS

For Erik Erikson,
Who helped me be a less angry, neurotic parent

For Guy and Max,
Great kids, now fabulous adults, thanks for helping me figure
out Part One

And for Paige,
My companion through this whole journey. Looking forward
to Stage Eight with you . . .

ACKNOWLEDGMENTS

Many thanks to Charles Hyatt, Richard Barker, Bernadette Berardi-Coletta, Jane Pini, Paige McGuire Martino, all the various Martinos (Mark, Kathy, Tom, Chris, Judy, Guy, Max), Martino outlaws (José, Steve, Barb, Mario, Greg), McGuires (Bill, Ruth, Michele), Katzmanns (Cierra, Reed, Shyanne), and the Fort Collins Senior Center Writers Group for being encouraging readers of early drafts of this manuscript.

PREFACE
IT'D BE HELPFUL TO KNOW THIS SHIT

You wanna know how to be a good parent? Here ya go:

Dr. Dave's Two Simple Steps to Being a Good Parent:
   Step 1: Be a good person.
   Step 2: Repeat Step 1.

Voilà. That's it. Go home. Be fruitful and multiply. Don't ask me how to be a good person. That's your job. You don't need anyone to tell you how to be a good person. As the saying goes, if you meet the Buddha on the road, kill him—figure it out for yourself.

[Brief pause as I realize, if that were all you had to do, I could stop writing now]

I'm not gonna stop writing. It's apparent that being a parent has always been and will forever be fodder for interest and conversation. When I was a practicing psychologist answering to "Dr. Dave," I discovered that everyone wants to talk about parenting but no one wants to talk about their own parenting, and how dare you infer I'm not the perfect parent and I can't believe you think I screwed up my child because I'm smothering or unavailable or overcontrolling or permissive or coddling or strict or, as Yul Brynner in *The King and I*[1] would say, "Et*cet*era, et*cet*era, et*cet*era . . ."

OK, maybe we could all use some help now and then. Go ahead, take a look at a hundred different parenting books, get a hundred different, mostly good, ideas. You can read about this or that intervention or those seven-and-a-half highly effective strategies and you'll be a better parent. You'll know how to deal with concrete behaviors and specific situations.

This is not that parenting book. This is more of a *meaning* book (but I wouldn't be a shrink worth my salt if I didn't add my two cents—or $183/hour—from time to time). If you want to be able to respond in a more calm and intuitive manner when you're in the middle of the transactional whirlwind between you and your kid, this or that technique will matter less than knowing, *Why is this happening?*

When I was a shaggy-haired, eager-to-please, neophyte graduate student in clinical-developmental psychology, my advisor said I needed to learn Erik Erikson's theory. Erik Erikson is THE MOST IMPORTANT WRITER TO KNOW IF YOU WANT TO BE A PARENT. Maybe that's hyperbolic. But, NO IT'S NOT.

Coincidentally, around this time my wife and I were having babies, a couple of bouncing boys. I found that knowing which Eriksonian stage my boys were experiencing

---

1. Warning: Possible Boomer references ahead. Look 'em up. Or not.

helped me better understand the challenging and borderline crazy behavior I was seeing from them. I'd read books and articles for my classes and research, go home and see it all come to life. I lost track of the number of times I'd watch my boys do something and I'd think, *Erikson friggin' nailed it.*

So who was this Erik Erikson dude who seemed to know why my kids were doing what they were doing? He was born in Frankfurt, Germany, in 1902. He generated one of the most robust theories of human development, despite the fact his biological father abandoned him before he was born and he was raised by his single mother, a young Jewish woman named Karla. It's never easy being born to a young single mother, and especially not in 1902.

Erikson persevered through a rough early life and eventually went to study psychoanalysis at a school in Vienna, Austria, where there was this guy named Sigmund Freud[2] who was practicing and writing.[3] Freud's ideas excited young Erik enough that he studied Freud and was psychoanalyzed by his daughter, but it wasn't long before student Erikson found the Ubiquitous One's view of development as too limiting.

Erikson was skeptical of Freud's assumption that personality development hinged entirely on the actions of the family. Erikson had witnessed societal upheaval and traveled extensively, which led him to conclude that social factors impacted a person's development. Freud focused on the individual. Societal conditions don't fit neatly onto a couch.

Also, Freud felt personality development was essentially

---

2. Damn! Can't talk psychology without talking Freud!
3. And doing a fair amount of legal cocaine.

completed by age five or six, when the Oedipal conflict[4] is resolved. Erikson made the valid point that any theory of development has to cover our entire life.

Erikson says development proceeds through a predetermined unfolding of our personalities through separate stages. Progress in each stage is determined by our success, or lack of success, in the previous stages. Sort of like a tree. Nature has determined how tall it will grow, how wide its trunk will be, or rather, nature has offered a strong suggestion that this growth will happen at this time, in a certain order, if given a reasonable environment. If we mess it up somehow, cut off limbs and such, or if something catastrophic happens in its environment, like a fire, then we could ruin the growth of the entire tree.

According to Erikson, the life cycle is composed of eight stages. Within each stage, every person has their personal tug-of-war between two opposing tendencies. We're pushed and pulled and yinned and yanged as inner psychological forces wrestle with outer social influences. If you win your wrestling match, your development proceeds in a generally positive direction. If your shoulders hit the mat, this can impair your development in a particular area and adversely affect the resolution of future struggles.

Each stage is a **crisis**, which involves a personal and deepfelt need to reexamine old values. Who am I at this time of my life? The idea of crisis is broader than how that term is

---

4. The Oedipal conflict is where the child desires the parent of the other sex and views the same-sex parent as a rival. "I want to have sex with my mom but I'm afraid my dad will cut off my penis." It's at this point, when I talked to students about Freud, that I heard a collective sound that wavered between giggles and groans.

typically viewed (as calamity or catastrophe). The crises in this theory are more drawn out and less specific. This theory's idea of crisis is more akin to how it is characterized in Chinese culture—the Chinese word for crisis is the combination of *danger* and *opportunity*. Crisis indicates risk, but it can also offer resolution.

Within each stage, you have a certain developmental **task** you need to do, which involves all your inner psychological stuff and the external demands of the moment. The tasks contain two terms. The infant's task, for example, is called *Trust vs. Mistrust*. At first it might seem obvious that the infant must learn trust and not mistrust, but Erikson made clear we need to learn a balance. Certainly, trust is a great feeling, but we also need to learn a little mistrust so as not to grow up to be gullible fools.

Each stage has a certain optimal time as well. It's no use trying to rush children into adulthood, as is common among people obsessed with success. Neither is it possible to slow the pace or try to protect children from the demands of life. There is a time for each task, and if a stage is managed well, we carry away a certain virtue or **psychosocial strength**, which helps us through the rest of our life stages.

It takes a lifetime to acquire all the psychosocial strengths. Present and future branches have their roots in the past; later stages are built on the foundation laid in previous ones.

SPOILER ALERT: If you don't want to know how your life goes or where it ends, close your eyes right now and turn past the next page . . .

OK, now that those chumps are out of the way, who wouldn't want to know? I mean, c'mon. Here's your Life Map:

ERIKSON'S PSYCHOSOCIAL STAGES

Stage (age)	Psychosocial Crisis	Who It Mostly Happens With	The Good Stuff You Get	Unless You Don't (Bummer)
I (Birth–1) **Baby**	*Trust vs. Mistrust*	Ma or Pa	**Hope**	Withdrawal
II (2–3) **Toddler**	*Autonomy vs. Shame/Doubt*	MaPa	**Will**	Compulsion
III (4–6) **Play Kid**	*Initiative vs. Guilt*	Family	**Purpose**	Inhibition
IV (7–12 or so) **School Kid**	*Industry vs. Inferiority*	Neighborhood and School	**Competence**	Inertia
V (13–24 or so) **Kid Adult**	*Identity vs. Role confusion*	Peers and Role Models	**Fidelity**	Repudiation
VI (25–35ish) **Young Adult**	*Intimacy vs. Isolation*	Partners and Friends	**Love**	Exclusivity
VII (35ish–60ish) **MAP: Middle-Age Person**	*Generativity vs. Stagnation*	Household and Workmates	**Care**	Rejectivity
VIII (60ish–death) **OG: Old Guy/Gal**	*Integrity vs. Despair*	Humankind or "My kind"	**Wisdom**	Disdain

PART ONE:

I'M OUT! . . . I CAN DO IT! . . .
LET'S PLAY! . . . SCHOOL!

Let's Get This Baby Cleared for Takeoff

Before getting into Erikson's theory, a quick note regarding the structure of these chapters. Each stage will be divided into three sections:

1. **WHY IT HAPPENS**: This section conveys Erikson's developmental theory in simple, understandable terms. He was a brilliant writer, but his prose was a little dense, especially for modern audiences—no offense, modern audiences.

2. **WHAT TO DO**: This section includes some of Erikson's thoughts about how best to succeed within a stage, but he wasn't big on handing out parenting or life advice, so I'll talk about some ideas from other sources, as well as offer insights I've gleaned from my life as a dad, teacher, and shrink.

3. **A POEM**: Hidden among these pages, in the poems to be found at the end of each stage, is my memoir, kind of like the surprise prize in a box of Cracker Jacks.[1] These poems were either written about my boys when they were going through the age under discussion (Part One), or written when I was going through the age under discussion (Part Two). Two books for the price of one! What a value!

---

1. See footnote #1 from the preface.

Far Be It From Me to Tell You How to Read This Book

Let me tell you how to read this book. You could chug it down all at once like you're a friggin' *teenager!* Or you could let me, your reading sommelier, recommend something—I know this vintage, it's a good year.

First, hold the book in your hands[2] and think, *This better make me smarter.* Open it and take a big sniff (literally and figuratively), really get your nose in there, figure out kinda what it's about, then take a swig, swish it around, and when you're ready, really read it.

If you have a kid between the ages of one day and thirteen years, don't dawdle getting through Part One—it's good to have a map of what to expect, and this is the best one around. Read Part Two to reflect on where you've been, where you are, and what's ahead. Return to the book as much as you like, see if these stages still make sense as you and your kid get older. If it takes a lifetime to read this book, that's OK, just be sure to read other books too.

Now swallow, taste, and . . .

---

2. If you're receiving this information digitally or through other senses, *imagine* a book in your hands.

STAGE ONE: TRUST VS. MISTRUST

(BIRTH TO 1 YEAR OLD)

WHY IT HAPPENS

Eat, Sleep, Crap, Repeat

Baby first shows **trust** by how well they eat, how deeply they sleep, and how regularly they crap. Simple. Eat, sleep, crap, repeat. Baby stays awake for more and more hours and all these sensations and feelings become more and more familiar, and familiar feels good—this offsets those bad feelings that occur when their bowels are working through a particularly nasty poop or their brain glitches as it comes slowly online.

If Baby can let Ma and Pa (which I will hereafter in this writing render as the self-made colloquial MaPa[1]) out of sight without falling into a rage, give Baby their first Social

---

1. I recognize and respect that many families are headed by one parent, or two parents of the same gender, or hundreds of parents with hundreds of genders, but I'm a very slow typist and "MaPa" has fewer keystrokes.

Achievement award. MaPa's (hopefully mostly) consistent behavior toward Baby has become an inner consistency within Baby. MaPa exists even if Baby can't see 'em. That's a big deal. So big that it can be considered Baby's nascent sense of identity, their first sense of who they are (more about this in Stage Five).

Trust isn't only about MaPa being there when needed, it also refers to Baby's ability to trust *themself*. Baby needs to figure out that when they eat, they'll become full; when they sleep, they'll wake rested; when they get that scrunchy feeling in their tummy, they'll find relief by shitting themself.

Make the Pain Go Away!

This trust stuff comes to a head for Baby between four and seven months old, when Baby's first tooth begins to push against their gum-line, commonly referred to as teething. Baby's excruciating pain is emanating from within themself, their own teeth, and no one, including—and especially—MaPa, can stop it. Sure, MaPa will go to the drugstore and get some tooth pain medicine (basically baby cocaine), but it doesn't completely get rid of the horrible, persistent throb that accompanies getting your first set of choppers. Trust is dinged by **mistrust.**

Teething is Baby's first Hero's Journey.[2] Before teething, if Baby felt discomfort, MaPa would rush in with the antidote: Hungry? Here, have some milk! Tummy feel tight? Let me burp you! Tired? Here's your crib, go to sleep, don't worry,

---

2. Read Joseph Campbell's *The Hero with a Thousand Faces*. Campbell was a Carl Jung guy—you could say he was well Jung.

you won't die, I'll be six inches from your face in the morning! But with teething, MaPa quickly lose their superpower status and become just another couple of ineffectual ninnies who have NO IDEA HOW MUCH MY DAMN MOUTH HURTS! Then what happens? Baby has pain and deals with it alone. Baby doesn't die. It's the first time Baby solves their own problem. Pretty fucking heroic.

Because *Trust vs. Mistrust* is the first stage and because the stages in Erikson's theory depend on and build off each other, this is in some ways the most important stage of development in an individual's lifetime. Is everything determined in the first year? Not necessarily, but that which is experienced the first year will be the template upon which all future achievements will be measured.

Life Without Trust

Imagine a life without trust. How would you approach novel and potentially risky situations without trust? Answer: You wouldn't. Where would your anger go if you didn't have trust? Answer: Toward yourself. Bottom line—without trust, a person is going to struggle mightily to connect with others, and may feel lonely and depressed.

No one, of course, wants this for their kid, and the inclusion of these ideas in no way assumes that any parent would purposefully act in such a way as to make that happen. But it's important to understand both sides of the crisis. We need to know what to approach, and what to avoid.

Trust and Religion

One of the unique contributions of Erikson's theory is how it acknowledges the influence of society in a person's development. Each stage or crisis has a special relation to a basic element of society. The human life cycle and society's institutions have evolved together. In this first stage of *Trust vs. Mistrust*, the social element is represented by **religion**, which is often defined as trust born of care. Think about it: With religion, like in that initial parent-infant relationship, there is periodic childlike surrender to a Higher Power; there are constant demonstrations of how small you are; and there is the insight that individual trust must become faith.

There are many ways for this religion to be manifested. Being a member of a formal religion is neither a necessary nor sufficient condition for healthy development in this stage. Non-religious people of social action or scientific pursuit are sometimes more moral than those who go to church every week. So let's just say that if God is love, then call it love because love is an easier word to verb. Everyone has loved, it's more difficult to have God-ed.[3]

B.P.B.

These are Bullet Points for Browsers, which I shortened to B.P.B. because I assume if you can't read a whole subsection, you'll want a shorter subsection title too.[4]

---

3. Play idea: *Waiting for God-ed.*
4. That explanation wasted seven seconds of your time—Sorry!

- Baby shows trust by how well they eat, sleep, and poop.
- Baby has to begin to trust MaPa, but they also have to learn to trust *themself.*
- Teething figures significantly in Baby being able to trust themself.
- What happens in year one has an outsized influence on all future development.

WHAT TO DO

It's Difficult to Fuck 'em Up

From the moment Baby comes into your life you need to prepare them to be without you, and the best way to prepare little human organisms for the vagaries of life is to instill in them a strong and abiding trust—a trust in the people around them; a trust in themself to deal with what life throws at 'em; and a trust in the world-at-large to provide a safe and orderly place from which to have thoughts provoked and feelings expanded.

Those first couple levels of trust—Baby's trust in you and themself—depends on the quality of the relationship with the primary caregiver. As might be expected, this quality depends on being sensitive to Baby's needs. I can hear you ask, "OK, but how sensitive and attentive do I really need to be, I mean they're babies, they don't remember shit, right?" To which I'd respond, "I don't know what you have against babies, but yeah, even you, with your minimal attention span and limited sensitivity, would probably have a hard time screwing up a baby because babies are really resilient."

So, the first thing you gotta know—it's difficult to fuck 'em up.

No one has to be perfectly attentive and sensitive to Baby's needs, and actually a few screw ups here and there are not only expected but helpful. You change fussy Baby's diaper but they're fussing because they're tired. You miss a signal and fail to fulfill Baby's needs for the moment. These screw ups teach Baby the world is not always fair and predictable and life-affirming—sad but necessary lessons. Call it despoiling innocence, or better yet, don't, that sounds creepy. Call it complexifying innocence, because who wants to be Baby their entire life?

Treat 'em Like Your Phone

A lot builds off this first stage, but no pressure, because Baby can endure frustrations in this or following stages if these frustrations lead to an ever-renewed experience of greater sameness, and the most important sameness is your face, front and center, twelve inches from Baby's face.

Treat Baby's face like it was your phone. Look at it. A lot. Make different faces at it. See what happens. Sometimes Baby will mirror your look, sometimes they'll complement it, sometimes expand it. Sometimes what's in their face will have nothing to do with you and everything to do with what's going on inside their meat brains and sausage bodies. Keep swiping. It's fascinating.

Be the giant head on Baby's internal movie screen. When they're crying, be there. When they burp and relieve the tightness in their stomach, be there. When they poop, be there. When they wake up, be there. It's sort of the natural thing to do when you're caring for an infant—keep an eye on 'em. And be there when they need you. Simple, right? Just abide by the following equation:

$$Tr = C \times Ti$$

Trust is equal to *Consistency* across *Time*.

Self: More "Less" and Less "Ish"

This is simple but not easy. The most difficult aspect of living with Baby is that last variable—*time*. It takes a lot of time to "just be there." Your life becomes, in many ways, not your own. Up to the parenting stage of life, being selfish was OK, in fact, it was sort of necessary when establishing a sense of who you are (Stage Five). But now, being selfish doesn't work. Parenting is nothing if not self*less*. You're responsible for another human. That's a big deal. So that brings us to the next major proposition:

First Corollary to Dr. Dave's Two Simple Steps to Being a Good Parent: Grow up.

Baby grows whether they like it or not. Every day their bodies and brains stretch and wrinkle. But when you're a young adult (in Stage Six, when most people first find themselves with Baby), growing up is a more active process. You have to choose to grow up.

The most legitimate path for a person to grow up into a responsible adult is to become more self-aware. Know yourself. You have depression or anger issues? Figure it out. You had shitty parents? Figure it out, or you'll repeat the same mistakes that pissed you off when you were growing up. Get a handle on your selfishness and narcissism because the little human developing in front of you is an expert at finding your weaknesses and foibles. To be a good parent, gird yourself with self-awareness.

I'm biased—therapy can help kick-start your self-awareness, but it's not the only way. Figure out how to be brutally honest with yourself about your strengths and faults. It doesn't have to happen all at once—it's a lifelong process. But you gotta be working on it.

Baby Belongs

As if that's not enough to work on, here's the trickier part —you need to convey to Baby that there's something bigger out there. Baby's life is great and all, with all the eating and pooping and sleeping and such, but where's it all leading? You need to somehow get Baby to recognize they belong to a family, a community, a society. This is where parenting goes beyond simple permitting or prohibiting. You need to represent to Baby a deep conviction that there is meaning to what both of you are doing.

How to do that? Introduce Baby to the aspects of your life and your culture that are meaningful to you. Journey with Baby as you seek out essential experiences that communicate to them, *I'm happy and proud to be living in this particular place at this particular time.* Show Baby this wonderful world we live in, full of strange and familiar things. Let them experience tastes that are luscious . . . but sometimes bitter and sour.

Let them see color and contrast and edges that fuse into images which pulsate and move and begin to tell the stories we tell ourselves.

All this comes together in the head and psyche of Baby around their first birthday. And even though Baby doesn't have the language that's needed to form specific memories, there's a lot of emotional information that gets absorbed through their senses and turned into neuronal road maps that are used in much of future decision-making.

So be consistent. Be there. Be sure to kiss Baby every single night, more if possible. Be sure to tell them, "I love you." Say it more than once. Baby doesn't understand what you say, but they certainly feel it.

B.P.B.

- From Day One, start preparing Baby to be without you.
- You don't have to be a perfect parent (no one is). Baby is resilient.
- Be there.
- If you wanna be a parent, grow up. If you wanna grow up, become more self-aware.
- Say, "I love you."

I tried to carry over that habit of expressing my love as my son grew up. When he was little, at bedtime, we used to see who could say it the most:

"Luvyaluvya."

"Luvyaluvyaluvya."

"Luvyaluvyaluvyaluvya."
Eventually, I would let him win and tell him a poem.

BABYMYBABY

babymybaby oh whaddaya see?
whaddaya see when you're staring at me?
whaddaya see with your big baby eyes?
whaddaya see when you look at the skies?

babymybaby oh whaddaya hear?
whaddaya hear when we speak in your ear?
whaddaya hear when we sing and we cry?
whaddaya hear of the world crashing by?

babymybaby oh whaddaya feel?
whaddaya feel when you squirm and you squeal?
whaddaya feel when you suck at her breast?
whaddaya feel as you crawl on my chest?

babymybaby oh whaddaya taste?
whaddaya taste of the milky white paste?
whaddaya taste as you slurp and you chirp?
whaddaya taste as you squeeze up a burp?

babymybaby oh whaddaya smell?
whaddaya smell of the scents where you dwell?
whaddaya smell of the flowers and hair?
whaddaya smell in the warm summer air?

babymybaby oh whaddaya think?
whaddaya think as you soar and you sink?
whaddaya dream as you sleep in your bed?
what are the visions you see in your head?

babymybaby oh whaddaya say?
whaddaya say when we smile and play?
whaddaya mean when you coo and you cry?
whaddaya want when you scream and you sigh?

babymybaby oh what will you be?
what will you be as you grow to be free?
what will you do in your life and your love?
baby below us, baby above,
baby go flying
fly like a dove . . .

STAGE TWO: AUTONOMY VS. SHAME AND DOUBT

(AGES 2 AND 3)

WHY IT HAPPENS

Hold On and Let Go

In Stage One, Baby was (hopefully) able to establish a basic faith that they *exist* and that there is some sort of meaning in this life. Then Baby matures physically, begins to use words, engages in fantasy play, and demonstrates some self-control. When this happens, they graduate from Baby to Toddler.

Toddler, awash in the warm cocoon of parental love and a hopeful future, does a quick about-face and risks all that hard-earned trust by demanding choice and pushing back against direction. Why? For a little bit of **autonomy**.

If Toddler could write, they'd make little signs that say I AM NOT YOU and march back and forth in a very annoying manner. That's friggin' crazy town, right? I don't know if it's helpful to see Toddler as a sociopath, but there you have it.

Toddler has two basic ways of approaching the world—

they **hold on** and **let go**. Both of these approaches can lead to either benign or destructive ends. Toddler can literally hold on to MaPa to both give and receive comforting hugs, but sometimes they can hold on too much, burrowing themself into MaPa when both could use some space. Toddler can let go, let it be, avoid the conflict, and put away the toys. But sometimes they let go impulsively and destructively—ask any MaPa who has eaten with Toddler and ended up with food in their hair (which is *every* MaPa who has eaten with Toddler).

Toddler vs. Toddler

As Toddler literally stands on their own two feet, they need to be protected because they can hold on and let go like no one's watching, but they haven't quite figured out when to do which. And when they make a wrong decision, they feel **shame** and **doubt** deep in their little Toddler psyches.

When Toddler's bid for independence ends in failure—when they say they can tie their shoe, but they can't—it leads to a self-conscious feeling. Self-consciousness stems from the idea that a person is visible before they're ready to be. Toddler feels like they've been caught with their pants down. They'll bury their face, sink to the floor.

That famous Terrible Twos tantrum is, first and foremost, Toddler raging against Toddler. It's a shame spiral. When Toddler feels shame, they wish to either become invisible or to blind anyone who is looking at them. Unable to do either, they may lash out.

The shame Toddler feels can trigger self-doubt. Doubt is the sibling of shame. Whereas shame is about the fear of being exposed, doubt manifests as some unseen thing that threatens Toddler's burgeoning autonomy. Just a minute ago, Toddler was positive they could tie their shoe, but they made a mess of it, so now they begin to doubt themself about shoe tying. Left unchecked, this doubt may grow and threaten their confidence in other areas.

Shame on Shaming

Shaming Toddler doesn't work. Toddler already feels ashamed. Telling Toddler they shouldn't have done what they just did when they damn well know they shouldn't have done it only serves to drive them underground. They'll still steal the cookie, but work harder at not getting caught. Toddler has definite shame limits, and if those limits are reached, it'll turn into rage, which will be directed at whoever is convenient. If Toddler feels you've been a shamer, you're up first.

The quickest road to shame and doubt is when Toddler, instead of establishing self-control through the process of trial and error, is overly controlled by outside forces (like MaPa). MaPa need to recognize even though they'd love to save Toddler from every bump and bruise, they can't put 'em in Bubble Wrap.

Which is not to say that Toddler can be left to their own devices. They need to have their autonomy and free choice be gradually presented and well-guarded. MaPa need to be the invisible wires when Toddler attempts a particularly difficult climb. MaPa's job is to set the boundaries and convey, "As long as you do these things in this area you're golden, but if you go outside this frame, you'll have to contend with me, little Toddler. Play in the yard but not the street. I'll let you get a skinned knee but won't let you die because of your lack of consequential thinking."

Repetition Repetition

Toddler's way of learning is to be repetitive with their toys, with their books and visual media, and with the people in their environment. Anyone who has been with Toddler for even a moment has heard the phrase, "Do it again." Toddler needs the freedom to really take possession of something—an emotion, an image, a toy—and test it, and then retest it. They're being little scientists.

If Toddler doesn't have opportunities to be free within constraints, that repetition may begin to work against them. Instead of repeating things to learn something new or to reinforce a favorite thought or emotion, they'll repeat things just to repeat things. They'll become obsessed with their own inward-directed repetitiveness. They may develop stereotypies—ritualistic, purposeless, and often rhythmic behaviors such as hand flapping, head nodding or rocking, pacing or spinning, finger tapping or drumming, or repetitive vocalizations such as humming or clicking.

Some stereotypies are normal for Toddler. They tend to do a lot of "stimming" (a.k.a. self-stimulating behaviors), especially during times of boredom or stress. When these types of patterns represent the vast majority of Toddler's behavioral repertoire, it may indicate an underlying problem, such as a spectrum disorder. If this is the case, the earlier the intervention, the better the outcome.[1]

---

1. This is advice from Temple Grandin, a brilliant woman who had an early

Not all such behaviors indicate the presence of a disorder, but repetitiveness will tend to shrink the range of what Toddler allows themself to do. This narrow bandwidth of behavior may gain them some control, but it's a small, hollow victory. They don't learn to self-regulate. This can lead to anxiety and OCD[2] kind of stuff or, less diagnostically, people who are apt to be governed by the letter, rather than spirit, of the law.

Law and Order STU (Special Toddler Unit)

No surprise that the social manifestation of this stage is the principle of **law and order** (not the TV series). Toddler is learning to balance the rights of the individual (themself) with the rights of society (MaPa). Toddler starts to see the limitations to their privilege and independence. It is during this stage that Toddler begins to establish a primitive sense of justice.

Toddler screws up a lot, but it's necessary. It's gotta happen. Toddler gives us a good life lesson: If you never test yourself, you never grow. Toddler is self-testing more than testing you, but make no mistake, Toddler is testing you too. If, when they're helping you in the garden and inadvertently step on every single flower you just planted, you're able to avoid making them feel shitty, they'll eventually get some of

---

diagnosis of autism and went on to earn her PhD in animal husbandry (and create a humane design to slaughter cows that is still in use). Her book *Thinking in Pictures* is recommended reading for anyone who wants to know more about how an autistic person thinks.

2. Obsessive-Compulsive Disorder (does obsessive-compulsive have a hyphen??).

their impulses under control, and this will lead to a lasting sense of good will and pride.

B.P.B.

- Toddler puts the trust they earned in Stage One to the test and demands autonomy.
- Toddler likes to hold on and let go—sometimes that's a good thing, sometimes it's not.
- Toddler's tantrums tend to be shame spirals. When this happens, don't pile on.
- Toddler needs the space to do stuff (and often fail) —they also need constraints (but not too much).

WHAT TO DO

The Tubular Twos

Since these events occur between the ages of two and three years old (plus or minus a few months), some call this time The Terrible Twos, others looking for less negative nomenclature, The Tumultuous Twos, and what I call The Tubular Twos[3] because it's a wild ride where you wipe out a lot, but the times it works make it worth paddling out into that breach again and again. Like surfing, you have to be attentive to what's going on around you, and your head has to be in

---

3. Patent pending.

direct communication with your body as you try to maintain your balance in a changing environment.

This stage is all about trying to keep your wits about you —you're the hapless movie director and Toddler is the bad actor playing a character with multiple personalities bidding for their Oscar. Toddler openly loves you and hates you; they will cooperate with you and be a willful asshole; they will freely express themself and clam up and tell you nothing. And don't expect predictability—Toddler can go from one extreme to the other in seconds.

Toddler's world is mostly black and white, so as Toddler's parent you need to work in the gray. What's the right ratio of love and hate, cooperation and willfulness, self-expression and suppression? That means you have to put up with some pretty brutal shit from Tyrant Toddler—lots of screaming and *Leave me alone!*s and *I hate you!*s. Tough not to take it personally, but that's the task. You need to remember that you're less MaPa and more just a safe object for their ire as they strive to become more independent (we'll see this again during puberty in Stage Five).

My Toddler Is an Asshole!

Here's what's going to happen: Toddler is going to over-step their capabilities and fail . . . a lot. When they fail, they're going to experience shame and doubt. As adults, when we fail we may also experience shame and doubt but (hopefully) we have some strategies and support to temper these negative feelings. Toddler doesn't have any such strategies and they're not so sure about the support they have. That trust stuff is still brand new and hasn't withstood the test of time.

Through all that shame and doubt—and maybe because of it—they continue to be assholes. They don't have a choice. Toddler has to keep testing limits, that's how they grow. So your job as a parent is to protect Toddler from being overwhelmed by shame and doubt. Meet their hate with love; meet their violence with calm peacefulness; meet their willfulness with explication of consequence: "Don't want to put on your shoes? Then you can't go outside. Sorry, buddy."

THIS IS NOT EASY. Just like Toddler, you gotta find your balance too. You gotta put yourself through the same process. You need to temper your hatefulness and willfulness (and if you think you could never be hateful or willful toward a two-year-old, you've never been in the presence of a two-year-old). And if you're lucky enough to have a parenting partner, make sure to take care of that relationship. In the face of The Tornado Twos[4] there's no front that's quite so daunting to Toddler—and ultimately reassuring—than one that's united.

The Significance of Poop

This all comes to a "head" during **toilet training**.[5] Remember holding on and letting go? Now think about what happens when you take a crap. Yup, first you hold it, then you let it go. Baby had no need (nor ability) for such trifles—thank you Huggies. For Toddler though, the discomfort of poop in your pants becomes a literal pain in the ass.

Enough has been written about *how* to toilet train Toddler.

---

4. Patent pending on this one too.
5. Head is another name for toilet, but you knew that.

It's more important to know *why* to toilet train. Toddler has to figure out how to hold onto their poop and when to let go. These skills of how to hold on and when to let go will figure significantly in the next (and all following) stages.

Most of the literature on toilet training comes down to one basic issue: Should the training be left to Toddler drawing on their sense of developmental readiness, or should the training be left in the hands of trainers, i.e., MaPa, and some sort of training program? The answer, as the answer has been throughout this stage, is that you need to find a balance.

If you try to toilet train Toddler before they're ready, they will most likely hold on because that's the best way for them to establish that they, not MaPa, are in control. Or if MaPa do little or nothing to encourage toilet training, then Toddler will likely let go indiscriminately, which means you'll be smelling that pungent Toddler poop at the most unlikely and inconvenient times.

As teething represents a significant issue in infancy (Baby's first experience of not being able to be soothed and having to soothe themself), toilet training has that kind of significance in toddlerhood. Toilet training symbolizes the classic psychological conflict between individual autonomy and social demands for conformity. And in this particular conflict, Toddler always loses. They must subordinate their autonomy to what family and society expect. They need to figure out how to poop without making a mess.

This dichotomy between autonomy and conformity is, again, solved by finding a balance. The vast majority of experts agree that toilet training combines waiting until Toddler is ready with introducing toileting in a guided, systematic fashion. You can't hurry it, but don't wait too long.

B.P.B.

- You gotta find your center when you deal with Toddler. You gotta be the gray between their black and white.
- Toddler can be a real asshole. That's their job. They grow by testing limits.
- Dealing with Toddler is NOT EASY. Don't be shy about calling for backup.
- Toddler has to learn to poop without making a mess. You can't rush it, and it's not going to magically happen.

So who'd a thunk getting your first teeth or learning how to poop on the potty would be so consequential? That's life, and here's a poem about it:

EVERYTHING POOPS

Most of our lives go in pretty big loops,
What goes in must come out and everything poops.

You can, "Take a BM," you can, "Go Number Two,"
You can say, "Defecate" or "Go poo in the loo."

Whatever you call it, that gut-bustin' voodoo
Is something we all will eventually doo doo.

A baby of course poops its poop in its pants.
A dog has a poo then it does a quick dance.

A rabbit poos poo-balls it then likes to eat,
And ill-mannered vultures will poop on their feet.

But by far the animal's poop that's most rare
Is a wombat whose poop is exceedingly square.

It's not just us humans and beasties who poo it;
Also machines and some buildings doo doo it.

Cars guzzle gas at an outrageous cost
Then poop it all out in the form of exhaust.

Factories poop out their waste in their smoke;
It makes the air dirty and that is no joke.

Nuclear plants will make energy too,
But their fission creates quite a dangerous poo.

Most of our poop, though, is safe and of use.
Cheap gas and some compost can come from your
deuce.

Good poop can let you relax and unwind.
There's nothing like taking a load off one's mind.

If poop makes us say, "Hallelujah and Gloria,"
Then that's when we're in a state of poo-phoria.

So next time you're posting a pic of your food,
Do the same for its poop and see how that's viewed.

Remember when having your sandwich and soups,
What goes in must come out and everything poops.

STAGE THREE: INITIATIVE VS. GUILT

(4 TO 6 YEARS OLD)

WHY IT HAPPENS

Chase Me, Catch Me, What Did I Do?!

This-age child, who we'll call Play Kid, is clearly no longer Toddler. From Toddler's disparate parts, Play Kid seems to grow together both in person and body. They shoot up into a human for whom we see a more specific future.

Play Kid is more loving, more relaxed, brighter in judgment, more activated and activating than Toddler. Play Kid has a lot of energy, which permits them to forget failures quickly and approach desirable (and sometimes dangerous) situations with direction. Play Kid develops **initiative.**

Toddler's independence was about independence of action. Play Kid's independence is about independence of thought. Initiative adds to autonomy the quality of undertaking, planning, and attacking a task. Play Kid is on the make, literally and figuratively. There is pleasure in pursuit and

conquest. Watch Play Kid on a playground (their natural habitat) and you'll see a lot of catch and escape, attract and run.

Play Kid's passion about the things they are making—
whether it's a crayon picture or a play scenario—at times gets
the best of them. They have all this newfound power, but they
don't always have the executive capacity to deal with it, so
they begin to feel **guilt** about the things they do, or even think
about doing, that are morally out-of-bounds.

Play Kid's "I hate you" is different from Toddler's "I hate
you" (and if you're lucky enough to hear that phrase from
Toddler or Play Kid, you know you're doing something right).
Toddler hates you because you're standing in the way of their
goal. Play Kid really hates you, like no-holds-barred hates
you, and like all hate, it feels good for a fleeting moment, then
(for non-sociopaths) dissipates into guilt.

The Big Split

It's in this stage that an important, fateful split occurs—
between, as Erikson puts it, "potential human glory and potential total destruction." That's a pretty big split, but if you
spend time with a kid this age, you'll see there is indeed a lot
going on inside.

Before this time, Baby's and Toddler's sole instinct was to
keep growing indiscriminately. Now, Play Kid's psyche
becomes forever divided in two—they are stuck between
wanting to remain a baby, and wishing to become a parent.
Erikson called these two instincts the **infantile set**, which is
dedicated to that initial instinct to keep growing no matter
what; and the **parental set**, which supports and increases self-
observation, self-guidance, and self-punishment.

Play Kid's rudimentary parent can be cruel, suspicious, and uncompromising. As they try on this new parental role, they may overcontrol themself to an unhealthy degree. They can talk themself out of taking the training wheels off their bike because, in their head, they're acting like a parent—imagining the negative consequence of taking a tumble. They miss out on the risk and thrill of independence by overrelying on their ill-formed inner parent. And since Play Kid models their new conscience on their real parents, many of Play Kid's regressions or resentments are because they feel their parents are not living up to their supercharged expectations (a tough criterion to meet). If you're having an afternoon snack, you may get more than a little miffed when Play Kid cites your prohibition against eating before dinner and waves a judgy little finger in your face.

If Play Kid ends up with too many guilt experiences at this stage, they can grow into an adult who engages in denial and becomes overly inhibited, or someone who overcompensates, shows off, and sticks their neck out. This latter strategy can lead to psychosomatic diseases (physical illnesses caused or aggravated by mental factors); the person has had to over-advertise themself and now must live up to their billing.

Though this stage sees the development of Play Kid's moral sense, which necessarily restricts the horizon of what's permissible, it also sets the direction toward what is actually possible and tangible, and permits those early childhood dreams to attach to the goals of an active and healthy adult life.

Dress for Success

Play Kid looks toward ideal adults to help figure out and understand what's expected of them. They are exploring, in a very simplistic way, the idea of **economics**—what roles can I play to bring value to the world? Not only is Play Kid learning from MaPa, they are also imitating adults in society that are recognizable by their uniforms and functions.

When I was a day-care teacher for kids this age, the dress-up corner of the playroom was always full. Those kids were literally trying on other roles and responsibilities in an effort to more fully explore what being a parent really means. These more ordinary ideal adults are often fascinating enough to replace the heroes and heroines of picture books and fairy tales.

B.P.B.

- Play Kid adds thought to Toddler's autonomy and develops initiative.
- Play Kid is better at planning and attacking a task than Toddler was.
- Play Kid has a lot of energy and newfound power, but they can't always control it, which leads to feelings of guilt.
- A huge split occurs at this age—Play Kid wants to remain a baby, but they also want to learn how to be a parent.
- Play Kid likes to try on different roles. Their play is their work.

WHAT TO DO

Show Us Your Identification

Erikson uses this stage in particular to point out the "dangerous potentials" of a human's long childhood and the need to "guide the young while they're young." It's fortunate that at this time, Play Kid is ready and receptive to such learning. Play Kid wants to play with peers, learn from teachers and parents, and emulate all the adult ideal prototypes. Play Kid wants to learn everything everywhere all at once.[1]

Play Kid does this through the process of **identification**. Where Toddler was pretty good at imitating behavior, Play Kid one-ups Toddler and identifies with their target. Identification is a more cognitive process than imitation, befitting Play Kid's more complex thoughts. If Toddler sees you smoke, they'll pick up a stick and try to smoke it; if Play Kid sees you smoke, they'll think to themself, *I'm a smoker too.* So, as much as you need to be careful about what Toddler sees, you really gotta watch yourself around Play Kid.

So in the face of this little meat computer's vigilant surveillance, here is our next major proposition:

Second Corollary to Dr. Dave's Two Simple Steps to Being a Good Parent: You're Being Watched.

---

1. This has nothing to do with the movie *Everything Everywhere All at Once,* but I highly recommend it.

Incredible Hulk-sters

This would be pretty much all the advice one would need if Play Kid were just a mindless parrot, observing and stealing identities. But Play Kid is not a parrot; they bring their own mind to the mix. And that mind is mostly filled with RAGE.

Remember, Play Kid is being pushed and pulled between staying a baby who has their needs met by someone else, and becoming a neophyte parent who nurtures others and becomes that necessary cog for the continuation of the species.

No surprise that there is a lot of submerged rage at this stage. Play Kid has to repress (there's one of those Freud words!) their fondest hopes and wildest fantasies, and this can lead to some vicious mood swings—*If I can't be Baby anymore, I'm going to judge everybody else for their moral failings!* If Play Kid is using their initiative for this kind of moral policing, we need to throw a wet blanket on that shit. We all know adults who are self-righteous assholes—you don't want Play Kid to become one.

Play Kid's rage easily turns into all types of outrageous behavior. Your task as a parent is to figure out *why* Play Kid is misbehaving the way they are. There tends to be four goals to Play Kid's misbehavior: (1) **Attention** ("Look at me!"); (2) **Power** ("I'm in control!"); (3) **Revenge** ("You don't love me!"); and (4) **Displays of inadequacy** ("I can't do it!").[2]

Each goal demands a different parental response. If Play Kid is jumping up and down and yelling when you're on the phone, ignore them as best you can, then be sure to give them attention when they're not demanding it. If Play Kid engages

------

2. Check out writings by Alfred Adler, one of the most important (but mostly unknown) psychologists not named Freud, Jung, Erikson, or Skinner.

in a power struggle by refusing to eat their lunch, calmly state facts ("It's your choice") and let consequences happen (hunger is a powerful motivator). If Play Kid tries to make you feel bad with a well-placed, "I hate you!" see it for what it is—don't feel hurt, don't punish, and do your best to build respect when they're not being such an asshole. And if Play Kid says, "I can't tie my shoes," don't do it for them before brainstorming ideas and strategies that may help, and really reinforce any of their problem-solving attempts.

Do I Gotta *Check a Box?*

Before leaving this stage, there's one more thing to be discussed. While all this physical, cognitive, and moral development is growing together, Play Kid is beginning to figure out **gender**.

Like it or not, we live in a gendered society. Every human society has patterns of organization based at least partially on gender roles. The specific content of these gender roles varies widely between cultures. I'm unwilling to get into the debate of whether gender is an in-born characteristic or is constructed by social situations and cultural expectations except to say that (of course) it's both.

What's more interesting (at least to a developmental psychologist) is how Play Kid's view of gender roles grows over time. Play Kid uses their newfound skill of identification to figure out a *basic understanding of gender* ("I'm a boy/girl and will grow up to be a man/woman"), and *gender role standards* ("Boys/girls play with things/people"—these standards depend on cultural and family norms). Then Play Kid develops an *identification with the same-sex parent* ("I'm a lot like mommy/daddy and I wanna be like her/him when I grow up") and begins to establish a *gender role preference* ("I'd like to be a boy/girl").

So what to do? I dunno. The idea of gender is changing so quickly that anything written today will be outmoded in a week. It's best to say: Don't be encouraging or discouraging. Meet Play Kid's ideas about their gender with warmth and curiosity. Don't shut down or construct anything for them. Let 'em be. There's a time (a couple stages in the future) when this stuff will become very important. Patience is a virtue.

B.P.B.

- Beware: Play Kid is watching you, closely.
- Play Kid *identifies* with you, which can influence how they think, feel, and act.
- Because they're caught between wanting to stay little and wanting to grow up, Play Kid is filled with rage.
- Know why Play Kid is so frustrated. It's probably one of four reasons: They want attention, power, revenge, or they're giving up too easily.
- Play Kid is figuring out the boy/girl stuff. Don't get bent out of shape. Be patient.

Now Play Kid has to get ready for school!
But first some haiku:

KID HAIKU

I.

Ice diamond sparkles
Beneath steel gray sky cloud streaks
Kid pounds basketball

Oversized clothing
Hat over eyes, handless sleeves
Yearns to be bigger

Scores at the buzzer
Lofted on shoulders of friends
Shy acknowledgment

II.

Snow bumps are mountains
Stage for flights of fantasy
King Kid of the hill

Dashingly rescues
Cop soldier football player
Prince doctor hero

Infinite as mind
Story starts with "How 'bout I'm . . ."
Ends in victory

STAGE FOUR: INDUSTRY VS. INFERIORITY

(7 TO 12 YEARS OLD)

WHY IT HAPPENS

Build It and They Will Come

Ladies and Gentlemen, walking across the developmental stage and into the spotlight for the first time ever, please welcome . . . SCHOOL KID! [*APPLAUSE*]

All of Play Kid's inward-looking moral and cognitive growth sets up School Kid's entrance into life. For most kiddos that entrance is into school life, but it doesn't have to be a brick and mortar enterprise—it can also be a field or a jungle or a community or whatever, as long as it's a learning situation that (like it or not) tames and harnesses Play Kid's huge imagination to more impersonal things, like readin', writin', and 'rithmaticin' (or huntin', fishin', and weavin' if that's your culture's jam).

Remember Play Kid was thinking, "I gotta be a *parent*?!" when they were confronted with the concept of taking care of someone besides themself? School Kid's response is a more matter-of-fact, "I'm gonna be a parent, yo." Play Kid's idea of being a parent was pretty simplistic—feed 'em, wash 'em, put 'em to bed. School Kid recognizes that parents also do other things, like make money and buy things that help the family. School Kid understands that to become a real parent, they gotta learn how to provide because that's what real parents do.

School Kid has to figure out how to earn a salary but they're too young for real jobs, so they learn to earn recognition (which in School Kid World is kind of like their salary). They earn their recognition by producing things, thus School Kid develops a sense of **industry**.

To help them make things, School Kid learns about the laws of the **tool world**. Hammers, brooms, paintbrushes, athletic equipment, and spatulas can be a part of this toolset, but more often nowadays these tools take the form of brain power, reading ability, computer literacy, interpersonal competence, emotional intelligence, and vehicles (they're too young to drive but they do love their bikes).

As School Kid matures and gains confidence through this stage, their desire for whimsical play is superseded by a motivation to bring a productive situation to completion. School Kid doesn't want to stack the wooden blocks or have the wooden blocks represent something else in their pretend play. They'd rather use the wooden blocks to build a small boat (which I did during this stage—it sank, but it looked cool).

Tech Kids

Since School Kid is beginning to have a more realistic (though imperfect) image of their contributions to the larger community, it's no surprise that the societal manifestation of this stage is the **technological ethos** of School Kid's particular culture. No matter where you live in the world, at around this age, children receive some form of systematic instruction to learn the tools, tech, and work habits of their culture's "Big People." In modern societies there's a lot of specialization so it's best to teach literacy, the widest basic education for the greatest number of possible careers.

Too much specialization can cause confusion. School Kid may find themself fretting, *I only define myself by doing this one thing over and over again? There's gotta be more to life than this.*

Child prodigies are extreme examples of this specialization. Prodigies can climb to the top of their professions at a young age—look at Mozart, Clara Schumann, Stevie Wonder, and Michael Jackson (music); Bobby Fischer and Judit Polgár (chess); Marie Curie and Jean Piaget (science); Maria Agnesi and Blaise Pascal (math); Tiger Woods, Wayne Gretzky, and most Olympic gymnasts (sports); and many, many more.

Being known for something so specific at such an early age can disrupt the identity formation that occurs in the next stage. Figuring out who you are in your teens and twenties (when a person is supposed to figure out that stuff) gets complicated if an identity ("I'm a musician/chess master/scientist/mathematician/athlete/etc.") has already been assumed or thrust upon you.

It's OK to encourage School Kid's passion, and at times their passion can be quite narrowly focused, but it's important that they're valued beyond a specific knowledge set. This stage is a time of broad learning and skill-building, so that when the real work of forming one's identity occurs (in the next stage), they have all the tools they need to make smart choices.

I Suck

The circumstances of School Kid's life are becoming thornier and more complicated. The goals of their initiative, so clear just a few years ago, are becoming indistinct. Their social reality is growing exponentially at the same time that MaPa's role in their life is becoming vague and ill-defined. School Kid's school can be a culture within itself, with its own goals and limits, achievements, and disappointments.

The danger in this stage lies in School Kid developing a sense of **inadequacy** or **inferiority**. School Kid looks to other School Kids to assess whether they're doing OK. Can I read as well as Emily? Write as well as Henry? Add as well as Lily? If School Kid judges that their tools or skills are not up to snuff in relation to their peers, then they tend to pull back to a more isolated, less tool conscious time in their early childhoods. They regress. They may isolate. They may bully. They may sometimes feel doomed to mediocrity or inadequacy.

If School Kid begins to feel that the color of their skin, the background of their MaPa, or the fashion of their clothes rather than their wish or will to learn decides their worth as an apprentice, they'll have a tough time establishing a coherent sense of identity (again, more on that in the next stage).

Works Well with Others

There are no rages in this stage as in the previous stage, no aggravations of new human drives. This stage differs from earlier stages in that there's no swing from an inner upheaval to a new mastery. Big, violent drives are dormant. This stage is the lull before the storm of puberty.

However, this does not mean that little is occurring. Quite the opposite—this is a big, socially decisive stage. Since industry involves doing things with others, it's School Kid's first encounter with a sense of division of labor. They gotta figure out how to get along with others, which will be crucially important for the rest of their lives.

That said, for most School Kids, this is a joyful, vigorous time. The heavy fears and vulnerabilities of the earlier stages are behind them. Because of their work in previous stages, they have hope and will and purpose and, therefore, are able to enjoy the resources and opportunities of their communities. From the secure base of their families, they begin to explore more complex relationships with peers and other significant adults, for example, in sports teams, scouting troops, gaming clubs, etc.

B.P.B.

- After all the physical, emotional, cognitive, and moral growth of the first six years, School Kid is finally ready to enter into public life, which is typically school.
- School Kid earns recognition by producing things, which is called industry.
- All kids this age receive some form of systematic instruction to learn what the "Big People" in their culture do.

- School Kid looks to other School Kids to assess how they're doing. If they feel they suffer by comparison, they may develop a sense of inadequacy or inferiority.
- Even though this is a pretty calm stage compared to what's come before, a lot is happening—they gotta figure out how to get along with other people.

WHAT TO DO

Friends—Not the TV Show

At this point the wider society becomes important in helping School Kid understand the many meaningful roles in its technology and economy. School Kid's development is disrupted if family life has failed to prepare them for school life, or if school life fails to sustain the promises of earlier stages.

If MaPa give in too much to their fears and are too sheltering of School Kid, then School Kid never gets a real chance to figure out how to be in social relationships. Toddler and Play Kid had friends, but School Kid, owing to the fact that their big brain is wrinkling into a complex social-evaluating machine, begins to develop friendships. Don't underestimate the importance of these friendships. It's within these friendships that School Kid learns to be flexible and consider others' points of view; they learn social norms and how to deal with peer pressure; and they learn to form close friendships, which become the building blocks for adult relationships.

It's good to encourage School Kid to hang out with others. Support them if they want to be on a team or in a club. Monitor closely, as not all of these early relationships are going to be perfectly healthy, but there's not a whole helluva lot you can do to prevent your School Kid from socializing with who they come across in the neighborhood or school.

So teach them how to be good social evaluators and cultivate their gut. "When Liam asked you to do that thing that was against the rules, how did your stomach feel? What was the talk in your head? If it doesn't feel right, be careful of doing it." Remember that trust that was developed in Stage One? Now it comes back in a significant way as, "Trust *yourself.*"

School Daze

As a parent it's easy to be thrown off balance by the enormity of school's influence in School Kid's life. MaPa has had a pretty good run in the influence department up to now, but then this behemoth called school rears its multibodied head and MaPa's significance takes a big drop.

What to do? You can ask good questions: Is school teaching my child the proper tools? Are they allowing my child to have a variety of experiences and not become too specialized? What are the teachers' expectations for my child? You can meet your kid's principal and teachers and make sure they're sane, reasonable people who still have some passion for the extraordinarily difficult and heroic jobs they hold. That said, once you drop your kid off at school for the day, it's out of your hands, right?

Yeah . . . sort of . . . not really. There's a lot you can do as a parent to encourage School Kid's skill acquisition.

Take reading, as an example. Reading skill is the most powerful predictor of school success in a literate society. For a kid who can read well, school becomes a field of opportunity; for a kid who has difficulty reading, school can be a night-marish hellscape.

As a parent, you can encourage School Kid's reading skills by clearly valuing literacy and academic achievement; by providing opportunities for verbal interaction; by making reading materials available at home; and by spending time reading with your kid and listening to them read.

Boiled down to its essence, here's our next proposition:

Reading Corollary to Dr. Dave's Two Simple Steps to Being a Good Parent: If You Want Your Kid to Be a Good Reader, Then Be a Good Reader.

Read a book every so often. Talk to your kid about what you're reading. If you ask my grown sons about the family trip we took out West when they were both school-age, they'll say what they remember most was that I read *Harry Potter* to them. Try it. You'll like it.

Find a Nugget

Besides all this skill-building, School Kid is also focusing on how to self-evaluate. As mentioned before, School Kid is constantly comparing themself to their peers. Toddler and Play Kid observe and imitate their peers, but this is mostly out of curiosity or to learn new strategies for approaching a task.

School Kid's pressure to conform and their need for approval complicates their self-evaluative process. If the previous three stages have been resolved in a relatively healthy way, School Kid will approach self-evaluation with confidence; if they haven't had a good go in those first three stages, their self-evaluation will be smothered in doubt.

School Kid's central job is to try to embrace their ability to make and do things while holding their feelings of inferiority at bay.[1] Too often School Kid ends up saying or thinking, "I'm worthless." What to do then?

I had to respond to that "I'm worthless" statement a lot as a practicing therapist and to do so I would typically utilize a strategy I learned at a seminar many years ago,[2] which consisted mostly of the phrase, "Pull for nuggets." A "nugget" is a positive characteristic a person possesses or something they do especially well. It can't be something general like, "But you're a good person!" The nugget has to be something tangible and specific to that person.

It sounds simplistic, but it was good advice. I don't like to use absolute words, but in this case I will—I *never* failed to find a nugget. Some people hid their nuggets pretty well, but I always found some.

Find School Kid's nuggets. When they're in their woe-is-me loop, or even when they're not, hand them a nugget or two: "Caleb, I like how you complimented Oliver on his shirt. You're a really good friend"; "Olivia, what a clever way to use that spare wood. You're a good builder." Make sure they

---

1. Spoiler alert: Those feelings never go away.
2. Mostly I dreaded the continuing education I had to complete to keep my clinical psychology license up-to-date. The vast majority of said education was an exercise in how to entertain myself while being bored out of my skull.

understand that they are more than just the sum of their parts. Make sure they know they contain multitudes.

B.P.B

- School Kid learns a lot, good and bad, from their friendships.
- Help School Kid be a good social evaluator; help them learn how to trust themself.
- School becomes important for this age kid; parental influence takes a tumble.
- If you want your kid to be a good reader, then be a good reader.
- School Kid often feels crappy about themself. Don't be shy about telling them what you like about them.

This brings us to the end of Part One. Let's get to Part Two. But first, a poem about getting along with others:

The Girl Who Fell From The Sky

There once was a girl who fell from the sky,
who landed like feathers (she knew how to fly).

There once was a boy who lived in the sea
and spoke pretty poems (but spoke them off-key).

The girl in the sky sang her songs without words
and the people who heard her mistook her for birds.

This vexed her, perplexed her, she grimaced and
frowned,
"I'm a girl not a bird, I'm a song not a sound!"

But alone with her dreams in the middle of night,
she doubted herself and she knew they were right.

"I'm tired," she thought, "of my static-y chatter.
I want to sing songs about stories that matter."

Meanwhile . . . The boy with the words all alone in
the sea
cast his eyes to the sky to see what he could see.

He was waiting for something, he didn't know what,
he had sat much too long in his comfortable rut.

The words that he spoke were trapped in a sphere
and bubbled around him and popped in his fear.

So he sat sad and lonely, watched water bend light,
and dreamed of the day as he longed for the night.

Then the boy who was sitting alone in the sea
formed a word with his lips and he let it go free.

It snuggled in bubbles and rose to the top,
popped out of the water, it just didn't stop.

While the girl in the tree, still singing away
(still looking for something important to say),

saw a silvery bubble rise out of the sea
and it floated on wind to her seat in the tree.

The bubble bobbed big right in front of the girl.
She could see all the colors in each swirling twirl,

all purple and blue and lemonlimegreen and
yellow so mellow and red tangerine,

it looked ripe and juicy, she took a big BITE,
it BURST, and then to the small girl's delight,

out POPPED a word, it danced in the breeze,
and she heard a small voice (off-key) whisper, "Peace."

So . . . The girl took the word and she said, "This is
mine,"
and it gave every note that she sang a bright shine

of colors of rainbows and chorus of choirs
and cool as the ocean and hot as the fires

and dark welcomed light as old foes left their cover
to join arm-in-arm and sing songs with each other.

The boy in the sea all alone in his bed
heard a chorus of voices sing loud overhead.

He swam to the top and chased down the sound
and heard his word "peace" rising high above ground.

The boy-fish was happy to hear this peace ditty
and wondered just who made his small word so pretty.

Then all of a sudden, he looked in the sky
and saw a small girl (who knew how to fly).

He laughed and he cried as the girl-bird flew by
trailing ribbons of rainbow of sound 'cross the sky.

The boy let the sound heal the hole in his soul
and forever felt happy and peaceful and whole.

There was a small girl (she knew how to fly),
and there was a boy-fish whose mind saw the sky.

PART TWO:

WHO AM I? . . . WHO ARE YOU?! . . .
HELP! . . . LET'S DIE.

Why'd Ya Stop Here?

I've learned as an enthusiastic cyclist that when you're on an adventure, every so often you need to find a nice stopping place along the trail to sit down and have some water and watch the world go by. This is your calm, shady place before the *Sturm und Drang*[1] of Pubertyville. Have a snack.

Phew! Those first twelve years were a lot, amirite? Half of Erikson's theory—Stages One to Four of eight—is expended on those first twelve years because more happens developmentally those first twelve years than any other twelve years of a person's life.

Many cultures have different coming-of-age traditions. In parts of China and Japan, these rituals typically take place when a person is twenty (which in Japan is also when they get to vote and drink). In Amish tradition, Rumspringa marks the time when a youngster turns sixteen and they are finally able to enjoy unsupervised weekends away from family and are encouraged to do whatever they please. In America, the sixteenth birthday is sort of a big deal,[2] since it's the age a young person typically learns to drive a car, get a job, and assume other adult rights and responsibilities. In Central and South America, young girls celebrate their Quinceañera when they turn fifteen, complete with a mass and a fiesta.

I was raised Catholic and had my confirmation when I was around eleven or twelve years old, which seems a bit

---

1. *Storm and Stress* for those who didn't take high school German.
2. The worst of these birthday excesses were documented for ten years on MTV's reality show *My Super Sweet 16,* which I will summarize with one word—*ugh!*

young.[3] Confirmation is the Catholic church's child-to-adult ritual, but the age at which this occurs can vary widely, sometimes as early as age seven. The Church has traditionally understood the age of reason to be seven. Does a seven-year-old really have a clear understanding of how the world works? (Hint: No!).

For my money—and for this theory's money—Jewish tradition gets it right. The Jewish ritual of bar and bat mitzvahs, where young Jewish boys and girls demonstrate their commitment to their faith and are responsible for following Jewish law, happens when they are thirteen years old (twelve for Orthodox girls). Thirteen seems to be a pretty good time to celebrate the transition from child to young person.

What we have left standing at thirteen is what I like to call a psychological homunculus. Ahhh . . . Look at 'em . . . Ain't they cute? . . . And fucking terrifying? They've grown like gangbusters and learned rudimentary yet powerful skills. They're mobile and literate, which feeds their self-sufficiency. They have tools to build things, literally and figuratively (these tools will be wielded as weapons when they reach Pubertyville).

If all has gone as planned, they're hopeful about the future; they have the will to challenge themselves and those around them; they have the purpose to undertake a task, and the competence to bring that task to completion.

All that being said, little time has elapsed since they've been unable to wipe their own butts, so they're still just kids who don't know who they are.

---

3. To demonstrate my maturity at that age, I chose my confirmation name—Peter—because I sort of liked Peter Tork from The Monkees.

What Part Two Is About

You may have read Part One to understand your own kid a little better, and if so, CONGRATULATIONS! Being curious about child development automatically qualifies you for Good Parent status.

Part Two is about life after a person's thirteenth birthday. Up to thirteen, parents have loomed large in a kid's sphere of influence. If you've been a moderately-invested parent, e.g., attended a least 75 percent of your kid's conferences, performances, games, recitals, concerts, breakdowns, joys, faux graduations (you don't "graduate" from kindergarten!), etc., then you've enjoyed a fair amount of influence over this wannabe human you've lived with for twelve years.

When you consider the graph of a parent's influence on their kid's development across time, it's highest at Day One because at that point the tiny alien-baby WILL DIE if not for parent's caretaking. That's a lot of influence.

From that peak your parental influence gradually decreases because, genius parent that you are, you've incorporated the information from Part One and used your time with your little critter to help them become independent in thought and action and, therefore, more and more comfortable being without you.

Then . . . [*Cue dramatic music*] a kid becomes . . . [*Mental video clip: Close-up of eye roll*] a TEEN! [*Sound Effects: Screams; door slamming; cries*]. They enter high school (or a culture's high school equivalent) and parental influence doesn't just decrease, it plummets.

Where once you might've been able to predict your kid's orbit around you, during the next stage your kid begins their own orbits and your parental influence has nowhere to go but down, down, down, *dowwwwwwwwwwn* like a Felix Baumgartner leap into space.[4]

In the next stage, with the onset of hormone-itis, parents are reduced to being a punching bag to their teen's manic search for identity. Then teen grows into their twenties and they're off to college, or a career, a marriage perhaps. Whatever's in store for them you have to trust (there's that word again!) that you've given them the secure base they need to make their own decisions. If you've done it right, they won't need you.

Which of course is not true. Children, even when they're morphing into adults, need their parents, and parents need to feel they still play a meaningful role in the lives of their adult-adjacent children. But the variegated parental influence enjoyed during the preteen years changes. As the kid grows up, parental influence winnows down to a single, simple mantra: "I love you and I got your back whatever you do."

It's always (hopefully) been this way, but now, in Part Two, even more so.

Parental influence may wane, but human development keeps going. If all goes according to plan, a child grows into an adult. Erikson gives us a map for how development extends through adolescence, young adulthood, middle age, and old age—four stages that cover a huge amount of time in a person's life (from thirteen to death).

Part One was about sitting on a park bench with your

---

4. Search for the "highest jump from space" clip to see the exact trajectory of your parental influence after thirteen.

beret, pipe, and notebook (we love ya, Jean Piaget[5]) watching kids grow, play, and learn.

In Part Two, you may still be on that park bench but you're not watching kids. Part Two is about the person reading these words right now. Part Two is about (drumroll please) . . . *you.*

---

5. One of those child prodigies who became a successful adult. Read about his theory of cognitive development if you want to understand how a young kid thinks.

STAGE FIVE: IDENTITY VS. ROLE CONFUSION

(13 TO 24 YEARS OLD)

WHY IT HAPPENS

Happy Thirteenth Birthday!

Do you have a picture of yourself, mental or otherwise, on your thirteenth birthday? Go ahead, find it, literally or otherwise. I'll wait . . . Got it? Take a good long look at it . . . That was the magical fulcrum between the end of your childhood and the beginning of your youth.

The person we called School Kid in the previous stage is now a teenager. They're no longer a kid, but they're not quite an adult. This is a transitional stage between the boundlessness of youth and the reality of adulthood, so let's call someone in this stage, Kid Adult.

Kid Adult has bounced back and forth between the poles of the crisis continuum and has hopefully landed more toward the positive side of things, thereby establishing a fair amount of optimism, determination, and intention. They've also developed a good initial relationship to the world of skills and tools.

Then Kid Adult hits puberty and has a physiological revolution [*cue Lennon's screaming wail at the beginning of "Revolution"*[1]]. It comes on gradually, then like a tidal wave, and when the dust or water settles (depending on your metaphor), Kid Adult is left with a brand spankin' new set of working genitals—penis, vagina, and breasts, oh my![2]

The rapidity of Kid Adult's change echoes Baby's leaps and bounds growth. Kid Adult is Baby again, this time battling the tides of a stormy hormonal sea within them and with the craggy shores of adult responsibility directly ahead.

With all this happening, Kid Adult becomes less concerned with how they feel and more concerned with how they appear in the eyes of others. Because of this, they question everything they thought they knew.

Let's Get Ready to Rummmmmmmmble!

With all these ch-ch-ch-changes[3] going on, Kid Adult's psychic homeostasis searches for anything that has some soothing continuity and sameness. One thing that's familiar, for better or worse, are the conflicts they had when they were growing up. So Kid Adult ends up refighting many of the same battles of these earlier years.

If you've ever lived with Kid Adult (or if you've ever been Kid Adult, which you have because you're reading this),

---

1. Do I really have to footnote The Beatles?!
2. *The Wizard of Oz*? Never mind ...
3. Bowie. Listen. Revere.

you've likely heard (or uttered) these phrases: "Why don't you trust me?" (Baby). "You can't tell me what to do!" (Toddler). "All you do is make me feel guilty!" (Play Kid). "Why do you hate me?!" (School Kid).

There's a shit ton[4] of battling going on in Kid Adult's brain. When they tire of that internal conflict, they search for a worthy adversary in their zone of attention, and look, here's good ol' dorky MaPa. When they're not embarrassing Kid Adult with how lame they are, they're saying Kid Adult can't do something they wanna do. Fuckin' MaPa!

Davey's Journal

You'll note that the growing humanoid has consistently sought out models on which to base their lives. They've imitated (Toddler), they've identified (Play Kid), they've looked to adults to figure out their realm of possibilities (School Kid).

The development of Kid Adult's **identity** is much more than the sum of their childhood identifications. All those previous identifications are run through a prism made up of Kid Adult's growing libido, their particular set of talents and skills, and the opportunities offered within their increasingly complex social roles.

Kid Adult's sense of identity is fed by their growing confidence that the inner sameness and continuity they've felt in the past is matched by the sameness and continuity of what they mean to others (remember, Kid Adult is all about how

---

4. Equal to three buttloads.

they appear to others). This is when the idea of a career begins to crystallize in Kid Adult's brain.

Here is an actual excerpt from my journal when I was eighteen years old:

> *I just found out what I'm going to do with my life. I'm going to be a psychologist. There, I said it. Why? Why not? Hah! Excellent start. Anyway, I got into Vince's car tonight and he told me how much he couldn't stand Charlie. By the time he dropped me off, I had him convinced Charlie's a good guy if you get to know him. I also had sweaty-palms-turn-around-and-blush-if-I-see-anything-resembling-a-female Vince trembling for an opportunity to call Mary, an honest-to-God opposite sexer! It's incredible what you can do screwing with another person's mind.*

Ball of Confusion

The danger of this stage is **role confusion**. There's lots to be confused about during adolescence. Gender is reevaluated. Having a working set of genitals brings real questions about sexual orientation. And as if that's not enough to figure out, Kid Adult also has to be able to settle on some kind of occupational identity—thus my journal entry at eighteen.

If Kid Adult doesn't have friends and a journal like I had, they may become overwhelmed at the enormity of plotting out their life before they can have a legal drink. Kid Adult can become confused and feel like they're going in a hundred different directions at the same time. To keep themselves together, Kid Adult will over-identify to the point of losing their own identity with the leaders and heroes of cliques, crowds, gangs, or groups.

The military knows this, as do street gangs, and media advertisers, and, and, and . . . Any reasonable psychopath knows that if a person is confused, they crave certainty. And boot camp or a street gang or a political party or a religious sect or a theater group or a sports team or a role-playing game can offer that certainty.

Many (too many) take advantage of Kid Adult's willingness, in the name of identity, to give themself over to a group or ideology. Kid Adult's readiness to pledge fidelity explains the appeal of simple (yet sometimes cruel and totalitarian) doctrines, especially if Kid Adult lives in a country or belongs to a class that has lost their *group* identity.

Romeo and Juliet

Like the title characters of this subsection, Kid Adult can certainly "fall in love," and literally be ready to die for this love, but note the quotes around that phrase. Kid Adult "love" is Kid Adult's attempt to define their own identity by projecting some version of themself onto someone else. Their identity becomes clearer to them when they see it reflected back. It's sort of like identity echolocation. When Wrenna solicits her bestie's opinion about her new boyfriend by asking, "What do you think of him?" she's really asking, "What do you think of *me*?"

That's why so much of Kid Adult love is conversation. It used to be talking on the phone, now it's texting or whatever type of communication is currently in vogue. Break it down and it's a lot of talkie talk.

Cliques and Clans

Kid Adult can be remarkably clannish and cruel in their exclusion of those who are different. This exclusion can be due to factors like race or cultural background; it can be because of more personal issues such as a person's tastes and talents; or it can be based on petty and trivial things like dress and gestures that have been temporarily selected as the signs of an "in-grouper" or "out-grouper." This is most likely the reason why it's during this stage that one's musical tastes are locked in. What one hears when they're sixteen or seventeen or eighteen is the music by which all future music will be judged.

Teen-dom is a time of extreme clique-ish-ness. This intolerance is a defense against a sense of identity confusion. Kid Adult gets through their confused discomfort by forming cliques with peers who think like them. C'mon, be honest, if you had a chance to be around a group of people who always agreed with you or a group of people who negated everything you said, which would you choose? Once you're in a clique it gets easy to stereotype and demonize your enemies and their ideals, via *groupthink* or *the risky shift.*[5]

Above all else, Kid Adult wants their friends to like 'em. Kid Adult wants to be affirmed. Kid Adult is putting themself out there with their shiny new identity and it'd be nice to get a thumbs up. When Kid Adult comes at you with a new outfit, hairstyle, tattoo, idea, or philosophy, resist the urge to say,

---

5. Two well-researched phenomena which say that humans in a group tend to think less critically and make more stupid decisions than an individual human.

"You'll regret this," and instead, be gentle, this is their first real identity.

Kid Adult is drawn to rituals. Kid Adult favors programs and organizations that clearly define what is good and evil, what is helpful or obstructive. There's a lot that goes into this identity-building and they don't have time for wishy-washy shit. They demand the same type of certainty from friends and family, often testing others' capacity to pledge fidelity. Put up or shut up.

Moratorium

Adolescence is a moratorium, sort of a waiting period between childhood and adulthood, between a child learning morals and an adult developing ethics. Kid Adult has an **ideological mind**. They are drawn to those parts of society that offer big ideas.

Big ideas are not always good ideas. Kid Adult battles with apathy and cynicism as they try to convince themself that those who succeed in the adult world are the best of the best. If the successful adults in the world they're about to inhabit are immoral assholes, then what kind of future is that to shoot for?[6]

---

6. For people such as my editor Laura, who currently parents a child in this stage, this question has led her to her "most dumbfounded moments" as she tries to explain to her son how a person who lies, cheats, steals, and bullies can ascend to a position of power.

B.P.B.

- This stage explores what happens between youth's promise and adulthood's reality.
- The upheaval of puberty causes Kid Adult to desire experiences filled with sameness and certainty. Fighting with MaPa is familiar, so that's what they do.
- Kid Adult begins to formulate an identity, a sense of who they are in this world. To get information about this, they get hyperfocused on what others think of them.
- Kid Adult's tendency to overidentify with certain groups can, depending on the group, be supportive or exploitive. Be careful.

WHAT TO DO?

What "What To Do" Means

In Part One, this WHAT TO DO section had a decidedly parent-to-child focus. This makes less sense in Part Two, with parental influence making its plummeting descent. From now on, this section will be mostly about how best to meet the challenge of the particular crisis under discussion, in this case, *Identity vs. Role Confusion.*

This Stage Takes Longer Than It Used To

Erikson saw the transition from Stage Five to Six as the

transition from puberty to young adulthood. More recent research supports the idea that, in this information-dense age, adolescence and identity-formation drag on much longer than they did a hundred years ago.

I went through a lot of textbooks when I taught developmental psychology until I landed on the one I cite in the references. It's a great textbook to refer to if you want to put a bunch of meat onto the theoretical skeleton being presented here. The authors argue that two distinct stages of psychosocial development occur during these years—*early adolescence* (ages 12-18) and *later adolescence* (ages 18-24).

Early adolescence begins with the onset of puberty and ends with high school graduation. It's a time of rapid physical growth, big leaps in being able to think and feel more maturely, newly energized sexual interests, and a heightened sensitivity to peers—a crisis of *Group Identity vs. Alienation.*

Later adolescence picks up where Early Adolescence leaves off and goes another six years or so. The ages between 18 and 24 tend to be years of becoming more and more independent from family of origin as personal identity is developed—a crisis of *Individual Identity vs. Identity Confusion.*

It's important to update old theory as circumstances—societal and otherwise—change. A hundred years ago the required amount of time for schooling and training was shorter, there were a lot more opportunities to enter the full-time workforce without a high school education, and there weren't many effective child labor laws.

Today's late teen enters a workplace that requires more advanced technical and interpersonal skills for success. At the same time, the diversity of available jobs keeps expanding, which makes figuring out a career path more difficult.

My silly journal entry notwithstanding, I don't want to give the impression that an eighteen-year-old has to have their life figured out. They don't. I didn't. Even though I nailed my profession at eighteen, there was a ton of growth I made in establishing my identity—my sense of who I am—through my early twenties.

I abide by the Rule of the Rental Car: You can't have the keys till you're twenty-five, which makes sense when you consider our frontal lobes—the part of our brains in charge of important adult stuff like planning, organizing, initiating, self-monitoring, and self-control—aren't fully mature until about the age of twenty-five. So let's delay settling on who we are till we have our whole adult brain to figure it out.

Moral of the story? Relax high school grad. Give yourself a little more time to understand the meaning of it all.

Parenting's Last Gasp

Even though it's clear that parental influence decreases when School Kid becomes Kid Adult and decreases further as Kid Adult gets to their late teens and early twenties, MaPa are still (typically) in the picture at this time.[7] As mentioned, often they're assigned the role of emotional punching bag as Kid Adult looks for folks in their world that will take their angsty vitriol without walking away from them forever.

---

7. This writing tends to assume no major traumas—physical or otherwise—affecting the growing human, and a parent or parents who are relatively sane. I was a clinical psychologist for thirty years, so I know this is not always the case, but this writing looks at typical development, so I'm not spending a lot of time examining what happens in the face of intra- and interpersonal catastrophe.

What to do as Kid Adult actively pushes away, in both healthy and unhealthy ways, as they search for themself? There's a lot written about how to parent an adolescent and most of this literature is quite good, but I'm not going to give an extensive bibliography.[8] There are also some spectacular works of art—books and movies—that really nail this age.[9] Take a look at some adolescent-focused books and movies to deepen your understanding of this time of life. If you do so, it'll likely bring back memories, good and bad.

But here's the short, simple, and sweet of it: Parenting Kid Adult is not a whole helluva lot different from parenting other ages. It boils down to the two simple words that suffuse all of parenting: **Unconditional love**. Let me say that again with different emphasis: *UN*conditional love.

Kid Adult is like Toddler but with working genitals and a driver's license, so they're going to fuck up . . . a lot. If the love you give is conditioned on whether Kid Adult does the right thing, then your relationship with Kid Adult will be awkward and strained. If you can maintain some type of healthy connection during this time of active distancing, then as Kid Adult grows to Young Adult and beyond, you can use

---

8. You may want to pay special attention to Cline and Fay's *Love and Logic* books and anything written by Mary Pipher *(Reviving Ophelia),* especially if you have a teenage daughter.

9. Again, way too many to list here, but off the top of my head: Fiction books like *Catcher in the Rye* by J. D. Salinger or *Black Swan Green* by David Mitchell or *Cruddy* by Lynda Barry or anything by John Green; movies such as *Breaking Away* or *Dazed and Confused* or *Thirteen.* I fear that by giving such a short and incomplete list, it'll only encourage folks to be critical because I didn't mention their favorite book or movie about adolescence, but honestly, I don't care.

that connection to continue to be an important part of your adult child's life.

The Joy of Adolescence

Many people see adolescence as a time of turmoil, risk, conflict, and indifference to societal norms. I confess I reinforced this view when, in this section, I discussed the *Sturm und Drang* of puberty or likened Kid Adult to a grown-up Toddler. But there are other ways to look at it.

Adolescence is a thrilling time of life. Think about it: There are so many firsts—first real independence; first job; first love; first heartbreak; etc. Kid Adult social relationships are more varied, more complex, more intense, and therefore, more fulfilling. Kid Adult is able to think more deeply and intricately about all sorts of social, political, and spiritual issues. Kid Adult makes important strides in figuring out who they are and how they can contribute in this long life they find themself in.

Remember Baby's Hero's Journey through teething? This is another in a long line of Hero's Journeys. Kid Adult is asking some of the biggest questions anyone ever asks in their life, all for the first time.

So if you're parenting Kid Adult, go against stereotype. See this time as a joyful stage, because it truly is. It's a challenge to construct a sense of self that is meaningfully connected to other people and groups, but at the same time is authentic and unique. That's quite a narrative to pull off.

We all did it somehow. High five!

B.P.B.

- Adolescence and identity-formation drag on longer now than they used to in the past.
- Don't expect Kid Adult to have it all figured out until they have fully-formed frontal lobes (which happens around age twenty-five).
- Parenting Kid Adult is like parenting other ages except with an extra emphasis on unconditional love (with an extra *extra* emphasis on "un").
- This wildly interesting stage is chock full of lifetime firsts.
- Give Kid Adult some credit and leeway—it's not easy to create a sense of self that's authentic and unique. Way to go, Kid Adult!

Following are two poems, both written during this particular stage, but which show the differences between early and late adolescence. The first poem is another excerpt from my eighteen-year-old journal; the second was written when I was in my mid-twenties, casting a cynical eye at those still in early adolescence. As you will see, the two poems are quite different in subject matter, style, and tone. The low-grade embarrassment and shame I feel in presenting these unedited poems mirrors the feelings that occur throughout this stage.

You're welcome.

QUESTIONS

So many questions are stuck in my head.
I'm here in my bed with my brain turning red . . .
    Who am I?
        Who are you?
          Why oh why?
            What to do?

Tossing and turning my blankets are crinkling.
Listening hard I can hear my mind wrinkling . . .
    Where to go?
        When to stay?
          How to know?
            What to say?

A flash of lightning burns the sky.
The door crack lets some light sneak by . . .
    What's the fact?
        Is it real?
          How to act?
            How to feel?

A clap of thunder pounds the room.
A fog hangs off a pregnant moon . . .
    Is it me?
        Is it you?
          Am I free?
            Are you too?

The silvery rain is beating, beating.
The flash and clap repeating, repeating . . .
    Should I try?
      Should I give?
       When I die?
        Will I live?

Now gently falls the nighttime rain,
how softly on my windowpane . . .
    What's below?
      What's above?
       Will I grow?
        Should I love?

Soon all my questions turn to dreams;
close my eyes on this rainy night scene . . .
    Will I be?
      Will I not?
       Will I see?
        What I've got?

Inside my brain where the scenery's bright,
I feel a soft breeze kiss me good night . . .
    Is it good?
      Should I trust?
       Think I could?
        Think I must.

So many questions are stuck in my head.
I'm here in my bed with my brain turning red . . .
   Who am I?
     Who are you?
      Why oh why?
       What to do?

MALL HELL[10]

I wake screaming from a nightmare,
Shuffle to the kitchen on swollen feet
Where I'm greeted by the brutish stench of day-old
hamburger.
I suck down orange juice and a cigarette
Before scrunching under the sink,
Like Martin Sheen in *Apocalypse Now*
Waiting to receive orders to kill Brando —
The Mall. DAMN. The Mall.

Freshly bathed and wearing black,
A 3-D Rorschach for all who care to project,
I walk through the doors beneath trembling neon.
My ATM card leaps from my wallet into the machine's
cold steel mouth,
Scaring out frightened virgin bills to be sacrificed
On the altar of the Mall God.

———————————

10. This was written when malls were a thing.

I feel like I'm underwater.

Kitschy bubble concertos play on a loop.

I swim against the tide, gulp for air,

But roving everywhere are

Wild packs of teenagers, TEENAGERS, *TEENAGERS*!

They've succumbed to a communicable angst,

Adolentia dementia,

Shuffling and giggling and screeching,

Dirty mouths and clean bodies,

Tiny feet in clown shoes,

Yards of useless cloth draped over skin-encased

hormone factories.

The jewelry girl searches herself for a new place to

pierce

And says in her tinny voice through glistening steel

Piranha teeth,

"I wear a one but if I have to, I'll wear a three."

Acned vampires and James Spader wannabes

Are drawn to mirrors like moths to light

To practice new and better poses to piss people off

And when hair flounces as planned,

Life . . . is . . . good.

Every fiber of their being screams,

"Look at me! Look at me! Look at me!"

And when I do,

They blow it and gag on bitter self-consciousness.

I need some air.
Sayonara, Piranha Girl,
Au revoir, my Clown Shoe Teen,
Meet me outside to drown some more
In the cold harsh undertow
Of another Iowa winter.

STAGE SIX: INTIMACY VS. ISOLATION

(25 TO 35ISH)

WHY IT HAPPENS

Welcome to Adulthood!

The purgatory of adolescence is traversed, and childhood is fully left behind. Truly, everything that came before this time has been preparation—from here on out it's all about actually doing stuff. The next ten years or so will make up the life and times of (you probably guessed it) . . . Young Adult. They finally got the keys to their frontal lobes and they're ready to go!

Every time a stage is completed and a strength achieved, the developing human seems to find it necessary to test that strength in the very next stage. Baby put the trust they'd built on the line by testing MaPa's limits and loudly declaring Toddler autonomy; Play Kid added a whole world of thought and undertaking to Toddler's independence of action; and so on and so forth. As was mentioned in the preface, these stages build on and off each other.

That's what happens to Young Adult. Kid Adult spent a lot of time searching for and eventually establishing their identity. Now, Young Adult is eager and willing to fuse this newfound identity with somebody else.

All Aboard the Intimacy Train

Young Adult is ready to commit themself to real partnerships and they have the ethical maturity to honor such commitments. They understand that such commitments may call for significant compromise and sacrifice, but that's OK, they're on board. Young Adult is ready for **intimacy.**

As anyone who's been in a relationship knows, they're not for the faint of heart. If you really want to get close to someone else, you have to be vulnerable to them. Young Adult has to open themself up, lay bare their fears and sensitivities, and hope that the person they're connecting with won't trample on their unprotected heart.

Young Adult's relationships call for a lot more openness, more opportunities for self-abandon, more sex and orgasms. The stakes in these relationships seem to be higher, both physically and emotionally. As the frontal lobes kick in and thoughts become more complex, there is more understanding and insight about how the world works, more inspiring moments with teachers and mentors, more (often unsettling) self-insight. If Young Adult avoids these types of experiences because they're not ready or able to handle that level of vulnerability, this could lead to an unhealthy self-absorption.

One Is the Loneliest Number

The danger of this stage is **isolation**. This is where Young Adult avoids all contacts which lead to intimacy. Isolation, as one might expect, doesn't lead to a great outcome. It can supercharge a person's biases. Kid Adult certainly had their fair share of exclusions and out-groups, but Young Adult, if they're grappling with isolation, can develop a more mature, and much nastier, prejudice.

Isolation can lead to all sorts of mental health issues, such as depression and anxiety. If there's been a lot of isolation and withdrawal in a person's history, this stage may exacerbate these patterns and bring about a diagnosis of schizoid personality disorder.

Even if Young Adult is in a relationship, this doesn't guarantee that they'll negotiate this particular crisis effectively. Some partnerships are an *isolation à deux*—the relationship exists but it's immature and lacks real intimacy. Such a relationship protects the partners from facing this, and other, life crises.

The Birds and the Bees—Young Adult Edition

That good old parent sex talk typically occurs (if it occurs at all[1]) before or during the previous stage. It makes sense to talk about sex as, or before, working genitals appear.

That said, Erikson saved his sex talk for this stage because it's the first time "true genitality" (which basically means "healthy sex") can develop. Kid Adult sex, if or when it occurs, tends to be frantic, guilt-ridden, and riddled with self-

---

1. I'm still waiting for my sex talk.

conscious thoughts along the lines of, *What do other people think of the person I'm with?* Erikson called sex during the identity-searching phase "genital combat," which I repeat here because I have an infantile sense of humor and it sounds like a sort of sexual Thunderdome.[2]

For Young Adult, sex isn't always going to be great, but it's generally better than the sex they had in high school or in their early twenties. Because Young Adult relationships are more vulnerable and complex, the sex tends to include more trust, affection, mutuality, and cooperation.

The Climactic Turmoil of Orgasm[3]

I've tried to mostly avoid quoting Erikson directly but in this section his wording is just so . . . luscious. He says that with "the climactic turmoil of orgasm" comes "a supreme experience of the mutual regulation of two beings." Wow. I'm not sure exactly what that means, but I want it.

He seems to be saying that if a couple can have good sex, this takes the edge off the anger and frustration that results from all the oppositeness that occurs when two independent, strong-minded, differently-raised adults find themselves in an intimate relationship. If a couple is able to have some good sex from time to time, they worry about it less and will tend to have less conflict within the relationship. As a therapist who worked with a lot of clients this age, and as a person who went through this stage, I concur.

---

2. "One penis and one vagina enter, either a penis or vagina leaves!"
3. Don't Google this phrase.

B.P.B.

- Young Adult takes the identity they established in the previous stage and looks to form a mature intimate relationship.
- If Young Adult avoids growth experiences or can't handle being vulnerable with themself or others, they may isolate.
- Too much isolation can lead to prejudice.
- Young Adult likely had sex at an earlier age, but healthy sex doesn't really come about until this stage.
- Good sex takes the hard edges off a relationship.

WHAT TO DO

You've Got a Friend

If Young Adult finds themself drifting toward the isolation edge of the intimacy continuum, they need to work hard to bounce back. That's not always easy to do because this can be an extremely busy time of life. Even if Young Adult is single and doesn't have a family, they're probably busy establishing their independence and starting a career. It's easy to get paralyzed by the pressures of living, and these stresses seem to be multiplying exponentially during this stage.

Being single doesn't mean Young Adult has to be alone. They need to find good friends, and work to maintain the friends they have. The efforts put into keeping in touch with friends will seldom be regretted. As a person this age continues to expand the idea of what it means to be an adult, having a supportive friend or two as a sounding board and companion will help immensely.

Sex Tips From Dr. E.

If Young Adult is in a relationship during this time, or dating around, or just looking for somebody, that sex stuff will probably be on their mind . . . a lot. Erikson himself had something to say about the "proper formulation of sexual health." I'll put the actual quote in a footnote[4] and summarize as follows:

If you wanna really meet another person, you gotta conquer a fair amount of deep-seated fear and insecurity and that ain't easy. Not to mention, there's a lot within the individual and their culture—health issues, moral doctrines, opportunity, prejudice, temperament, and so on—that can absolutely work against getting laid. All we have for certain is the opportunity, but you'd better be ready and able to bear up under the blunt force trauma of loneliness and rejection without completely falling apart.

Check me. Did I get the gist? Whether you go to the original text or my summary, it's pretty brutal, right?

Who Hates Their Life the Most?

When I was teaching developmental psychology, I would

---

4. "A human being should be potentially able to accomplish mutuality of genital orgasm, but he should also be so constituted as to bear a certain amount of frustration in the matter without undue regression wherever emotional preference or consideration of duty and loyalty call for it."

ask my students, "At what time during the lifespan do you think life satisfaction is at its lowest? At what age are you least satisfied with your life?" What do *you* think?

A lot of folks would point to adolescence or old age as especially difficult times in a person's life, and I'd say, "Those stages have their challenges, but there's a good level of support and self-acceptance at those ages," and since I'm asking the question at this point in the book, I'm sure you're clever enough to figure out that people in this stage—*Intimacy vs. Isolation*—often report the least amount of life satisfaction.

It's a tough time of life, at least it was for me—old enough to get married and have a young kid but still slogging through the long apprenticeship of becoming a licensed shrink. Young Adult always seems to be running a low-grade impostor syndrome fever, especially when having to be an adult in the adult world. Young Adult has to suffer the slings and arrows of criticism and advice about how to be better at their gender and how to do sex. That's a lot.

Let's file this under Hero Journey #6. Every stage seems to have its own Hero's Journey, and this one is no exception. Young Adult has to take that leap into vulnerability and abandon while dodging and dealing with adult responsibility and rejection. Why would anyone in their right mind put up with that shit?

I'll tell ya why—at the end of this journey is the holy fuckin' grail of it all, baby! At the end of this journey is . . . **love.**

Cos'è l'amore?

Writers, poets, philosophers, artists of every stripe have had their crack at defining love, but for my money I'll go with the psychologist, specifically a guy named Robert Sternberg.

According to Sternberg's Triangular Theory of Love, all types of love can be viewed as a combination of three dimensions:

1. **Passion**—the libido-forward expression of physical needs and desires;
2. **Intimacy**—the emotional investment in a relationship that promotes closeness and connection;
3. **Commitment**—the cognitive decision to remain in the relationship.

Each of these dimensions vary over time and interact with each other. Passion is the most fleeting and red hot, but without commitment, this kind of love will be short-lived. Intimacy and commitment can grow over time and, depending on the level of passion, have the ability to blossom into different types of love.

I referred to this theory a lot when counseling couples or adults worried about their relationships. Often, I was met with the complaint, "There's not as much passion now as there was at the beginning of the relationship," to which I would reply, "Wha'd ya *expect*?" Passion is a firework—it burns brightly for a moment and it's gone. Can you still talk honestly and deeply with each other? (Intimacy). Do you still wanna be in the relationship? (Commitment). If so, you still got a lot of love there.

It's important to understand these dimensions so that we can have realistic expectations about the love relationship we find ourselves in. Of course, everyone wants consummate love—that's a love relationship with all three dimensions—but you can have a sturdy, steady relationship that's heavy on one dimension and not so much on the others and still be happy or content.

So go ahead, pay attention to all those romantic poets and singers and artists as you search for the true meaning of love. But while you're at it, throw a little research science into the mix so that you can truly understand the love you give and receive.

B.P.B.

- Young Adult can get much needed solace and support from close friendships.
- This is the age when most people report being dissatisfied with their lives.
- If you bear through this tough time of life and really work on being intimate with somebody, then you may get to experience, for the first time, real love.
- Love is multidimensional—it consists of passion, intimacy, and commitment. It's nice to have all three, but if you don't, you can still have a happy love relationship.

Now here's a poem about love:

Skeleton Winter

Cold night knifes through me like I was a skeleton.
Wax tearstreams crease my face.
I'm outta place.
      You're not here.
I hunch against the bad blow
Watch black boots kick my shadow.
You're not here so I can
Hold your hand
Like it had no skin.
      Let's begin again.
Fold me in your skeleton arms and
Sway me with your skeleton charms and
Let me lay forever on your heart.
      We will start anew,
Picnicking together under a dream,
Holding skeleton hands in moonlight gleam,
Dancing in the graveyard like kids at Christmas.
      I think of you.
I am told when nights are cold
Your touch will melt a frozen heart.
Reach through my chest as I kiss your breast
      And we will never part.

STAGE SEVEN: GENERATIVITY VS. STAGNATION
(35ISH TO 60ISH)

WHY IT HAPPENS

A Teaching and Learning Animal

The last two stages have covered about ten to twelve years each. This stage is, time-wise, the longest, covering the next thirty years or so. It's also the stage, along with the final one, with the least information because, like those before him, Erikson spent the bulk of his effort on the childhood stages (the book referencing his theory is called *Childhood and Society*).

That said, this stage is central if we're talking about human beings' evolutionary development. It's during this stage that we finally see Human Person become, in Erikson's words, a "teaching and learning animal," which is critical for the perpetuation of the species.

Part One amply showed that children are quite dependent on the adults in their life. Too often this obscures the fact that older generations are dependent on the younger generation.

As will be discussed in the next stage, older adults need to be needed, and as discussed in the previous stage, younger adults need encouragement and forbearance as they work to establish themselves. Middle-Age Person (who we'll call MAP to save keystrokes) is uniquely positioned to have influence on folks on either side of them. MAP is at peak influence with everyone along the developmental timeline. This is why MAP is seen as a member of the **Sandwich Generation**—they're often caught caring for people both younger and older than them.

The examples of MAPs in popular culture are too numerous to list. Some are figuratively (or literally) cartoonish, from the suit-wearing dad and dress-wearing mom of *Leave It to Beaver*, to d'oaf-ish Homer and long-suffering Marge Simpson. The best of these depictions touch on the complexity of MAP.[1]

Talkin' 'Bout My G-G-Generation[2]

The primary concern of this stage and this age is to estab-

---

1. Again, here is a woefully-incomplete off-the-top-of-my-head list (I call it, "Dave AI")—Movies: *Parenthood; Raising Arizona; The Pursuit of Happyness; The Kids Are All Right; The Mitchells vs. the Machines; Little Miss Sunshine.* TV shows: *Schitt's Creek; Black-ish.* Books: *To Kill a Mockingbird* by Harper Lee; *Beloved* by Toni Morrison; *The World According to Garp* by John Irving; *The Road* by Cormac McCarthy. John Updike's *Rabbit* books and Elena Ferrante's *Neapolitan Novels* are series that deftly show MAP's maturation through time. Because of MAP's centrality to all generations, these movies, shows, and books also have brilliant portrayals of people in other stages of life.
2. "My Generation" is a song by The Who which is really about people in stages Five or Six, especially with lyrics like, "Hope I die before I get old," but I've co-opted it for this stage because, why not?

lish and guide the next generation, thus the positive end of this crisis continuum is called **generativity**. For about a third of MAP's life, they've worked to learn things and establish themself—the next thirty years or so tend to be devoted to the idea of **giving back** their hard-earned expertise to other generations.

For the jobs I had, it was easy to see how that giving back manifested. As a therapist, I encouraged people to be more at peace with their lives; as a college professor, I taught young people about things I knew a lot about (clinical and developmental psychology); as a dad, I helped raise a couple kids from zero to independence. These ideas of generativity and giving back to the next generation clicked with what I was doing.

A MAP can be generative as long as they use the skills they've established earlier in their lives to be creative and productive. Sure, you can be generative by parenting a kid, but you can also be generative by inventing, teaching, creating art, improving the physical or social environment, etc. As MAP ages through this stage, there are lots of chances to mentor (teach) and be mentored (learn). The more open MAP is to those opportunities, the more generative they'll feel.

Remember how each stage seems to reevaluate and expand on the stage that comes just before it? Same here—the ability to lose oneself in the coming together (*la petite mort!*[3]) of minds and bodies from the *Intimacy vs. Isolation* stage leads MAP to expand their investment in important relationships and secure a healthy future. MAP loses some of the abstract idealism of their Young Adult phase and increases

---

3. French for "the little death," which is also what an orgasm is called.

their knowledge of all things practical. Their ability to navigate the often-tricky waters of managing a household and securing a solid financial future for themself and their family can be seen as a middle-age superpower.[4]

MAP is beginning to recognize their own mortality; therefore, they feel more compelled to make contributions to society, on both personal and public levels, that will stand some chance of continuing after they die. Society, in return, tends to support MAP's efforts in this regard. Most institutions, be they economic, philosophical, educational, or spiritual, are committed to the idea of improving the life of future generations.

I Can't Do It and Don't Make Me Try

If MAP is unable to find or invest in work or personal relationships, and if MAP can't move forward and find ways to give back to themself, their significant others, or their community, they may regress. A MAP who feels they're going nowhere in their career or who is overwhelmed with the chaos and responsibilities of their personal lives may search, sometimes obsessively, for pseudo-intimacy—relationships that feel intimate but really aren't. This is often accompanied by a sense of personal impoverishment and **stagnation**.

Remember this is a long stage, time-wise. MAP experi-

---

4. Check out "SNL Middle-Aged Man" on YouTube—an early '90s Mike Myers character who was between forty and sixty-five years old. He would solve a younger adult's problems with his knowledge of important but mundane things like understanding annuities or how to jump-start a car or how to file warranties on your appliances, etc. It was funny when I first saw it, but funnier now, having gone through it.

ences many complex challenges they may not be prepared for, e.g., being passed over for a promotion or being promoted to a position for which they're not ready; needing to care for an aging parent; dealing with growing family issues or, in about half of marriages, negotiating a divorce. Every success and failure MAP experiences brings them face-to-face with reexamining and redefining their goals. MAP may doubt their ability to move ahead or make meaningful contributions, which leads to surging feelings of stagnation.

When MAP is stagnating, they may begin to indulge themself as if they were their own child. This can lead to narcissistic displays as a defense against intense insecurity, or it can lead to paralyzing self-concern, a physical and psychological invalidism. Remember Play Kid and their displays of inadequacy? This is the MAP equivalent: "I can't do it and don't make me try."

MAP may think parenting is necessarily generative, but the mere fact of wanting or having children does not achieve generativity. Many young parents hit a wall in this stage because of (you guessed it) disruptions in previous stages. If MAP, when they are going through the *Identity vs. Role Confusion* phase, developed a self-made personality around the idea of, *I love myself and everyone else should love me too,* and if they hang on to that too much, this will hinder them when they become a parent—remember, parenting is nothing if not selfless. Or it could go all the way back to the beginning, where the young parent lacks a basic trust in their community to be able to welcome and help take care of their kid. Problems in parenting and generativity can have their roots in disruptions at any stage.

B.P.B.

- This is a long stage with a lot going on.
- MAP is a member of The Sandwich Generation—they're caught between caring for people both younger and older than them.
- MAP is concerned about being generative—they give back to the younger generation all the shit they've learned so far.
- If MAP feels overwhelmed or like they're going nowhere in their life, this leads to feelings of stagnation.

WHAT TO DO

A Life in Full

There are a lot of years here to account for and, obviously, who you are at thirty-five is quite different from who you are at sixty. That said, there are certain ideas and issues that crucially define what middle-age is.

This is the time when we blossom into the fullness of life. MAP is at peak influence and meaningfulness with people who are young, old, and everywhere in between, so first off, revel in it. Never again will you be so needed. What you do during this stage matters wildly to you, your loved ones, and the people you touch in small and large ways; therefore, it matters to the future of the *fucking world.* Use this time wisely. Don't take it for granted.

Middle-age is a person's time to change the world by

introducing new ideas, new relationships, and sometimes new people, all of which had not existed before. Though these ideas of generativity and giving back are most identified with middle-age, it's a skill that emerges over the life course. Adolescents and young adults certainly have ideas of how they can give back, but these ideas typically take the form of motives or aspirations. Middle-age is when these generative ideas are often realized.

That Word Again

MAP is the adult in charge, the fulcrum between young and old. You gotta have . . . what's the word I'm looking for? It means trying to steady yourself between two opposing forces? Hmm, I think I've said it before . . . Could it be, *balance?* I'm trying to balance the number of times I've used the word balance with the fact that so much of this theory, and of life in general, is indeed about balance.

Middle-age is the time when the phrase "work–life balance" becomes crucially important. The domains of work and family, both central to middle-age adult lives, are likely to conflict under certain circumstances. Sometimes work responsibilities spill over and interfere with MAP's family duties; likewise, family disruptions can make it difficult to meet work expectations.

If a job includes major responsibility, a high workload, and lots of travel, and if MAP's family life finds them married and responsible for kids and elders, they're going to be at risk for work–life *im*balance. In the uncivilized backwater country called the US of A, the potential for such conflict increases if you're female because (1) there still exists a significant pay gap between men and women doing the same job; (2) becoming a parent is more likely to set women back in their careers than men; and (3) the responsibility for household and child-rearing still falls more heavily on women than men, regardless of employment status.

Adapting to the demands of both work and family is not easy. There are a lot of interacting systems at play here—each partner's work environment, responsibilities within the family, and relationships with each other and their children. It doesn't take much for one realm to bleed, often negatively, into the other. If MaPa have to work long hours or feel overloaded, they'll have less energy, physically and emotionally, to deal calmly and rationally with the challenges of raising a kid.

How to bring positive energy from work to your family? This can occur if MAP is able to see work as a source of self-worth or fulfillment, which can be a personal decision, but more often happens if the workplace has resources that help their employees address pressing family demands within the scope of their daily work.

So when looking for a job, look for smart employers. A smart employer will have synthesized the social science research, which shows that if an employee feels confident that they're not neglecting their family, they make better workers. Does the company you work for have on-site day-care? Do they have policies that allow for family-related leaves without risking job security? The climate of the work setting has a lot to do with whether this work–life balance is achieved.

And sometimes it's a personal decision. My dad worked as a businessman at a time in the culture when progressive pro-family policies were barely a blip on a big company's radar. At my dad's funeral, I lost track of the number of his business colleagues who came up to me and my siblings to tell us how much they admired his commitment to family. Even though my dad rose to a position of significant prominence in his company,[5] he never missed a family dinner or a ballgame, he never worked on a weekend. If it was between spending time at work or spending time with family, family won out with Dad every time. That's a good dad and a good model. Thanks Dad.

The Airplane Metaphor

There's a lot of **care** involved during this time of life. If you have kids, you're nurturing them; you're helping your parents as they age, and your grandparents too, if you're lucky enough to still have 'em. All the strengths acquired from infancy to young adulthood (hope and will, purpose and skill, fidelity and love) come together and are essential to this generative task of caring.

There is nothing like the feeling of being connected and useful to another person. As the crisis of *Generativity vs. Stagnation* is resolved in a positive direction, MAP finds new energy and innovative ways to express their capacity to care. Whether it's being able to see your kid safely through the challenges of childhood, or helping the folks who raised you age with dignity, to be able to truly care about the well-being of a fellow human can be as comforting to the care-*er* as it is for the care-*ee*.

---

5. At the end of his career (before succumbing to the horrors of early-onset Alzheimer's), he was in charge of helping the large pharmaceutical company he worked for expand into different countries, or as I would tell my friends, "My dad sells drugs in South America."

Even though the rewards of caring are enormous, it's exhausting. Ask anyone who is living or has lived it—caring is much more difficult than indifference. It takes time, effort, and energy—physical and emotional. So what's a shrink's response to someone who finds themself caring for others a lot? Simple. Don't forget to care for *yourself.*

Self-care is always important but especially so during this time of life. I can't count the number of times that I found myself as a therapist sitting across from a well-meaning but worn-out MAP and telling them the airplane metaphor, to wit, if you're on an airplane with a child and there's an emergency and the oxygen masks fall, what should you do? Most sentient adults have subconsciously incorporated the preflight safety instructions they've heard time and time again and will say, "Put the mask on yourself first." Why? Because if you're gasping for air, you're no help to the kid. Take care of yourself if you want to be an effective care-er to others.

Self-care in middle age is an attitude which can be best summed up by the phrase, "Treat Yo'self!"[6] So here, in no particular order, is a brief, nonexhaustive list of things you can do for yourself:

See live music; see some stand-up; see a play; read a book; tell a joke; keep a journal; scream real loud; go for a drive to see the fall colors; go to therapy; go for a walk; go for a bike ride; climb something (somewhere between stairs and mountains, literal and figurative); admire trees; sit by water; plant something; eat, pray, love; eat your prey and love; order

---

6. This phrase was stolen from, if not the best, one of the best sitcoms of all time, *Parks and Rec* (Season 4, Episode 4). It's a phrase spoken mostly by Tom and Donna, but in this episode, also by Ben, whose ultimate "Treat Yo'self" gift makes me crazy-cry with laughter every time I see it.

dessert; be able to say "no"; delegate something; watch *Parks and Rec*; give a hug that lasts more than three seconds (if you receive such a hug that absolutely qualifies as self-care); watch a kid play; draw a picture; make something with your hands; have good sex; clear some clutter; get a cat (on second thought, that's *cat*-care not self-care); get a dog (I'm a dog person, obvs); volunteer; meditate; travel; prioritize sleep; eat in ways where you don't feel full of regret (either eat more healthy or let go feeling guilty about it); do nothing; [include your particular brand of self-care HERE].

B.P.B.

- MAP is at peak influence with people who are younger, older, and everywhere in between. Use this influence wisely.
- At this age, the idea of work–life balance is very important.
- Look for an employer who understands that you'll be a better worker if you feel you're not neglecting your family.
- MAP does a lot of caring for others, which can be exhausting.
- MAP has to *first* care for themselves, or they'll be useless to others.

Here's one more self-care item: Write or read a poem or two.

Following are a couple poems about the two most important ideas of this stage—work and family. The first is about work (a therapy progress note in poem form); the second is about family (with a title that's an homage to the great R. Buckminster Fuller[7]).

WALKING ON OLD SOULS
For Miss Bea Gotten.

She changes her moods like she washes her clothes.
Every day she drip-dries her melancholy,
Puts her anger through the SPIN cycle,
Irons her obsession with
Cool starch paranoia.

She comes home from another day
Of binging and purging on her pride,
With an attitude that says,
"No one can kick my ass as good as I can."

She is wide-eyed flutter, then,
Complete shutdown, a disconnected robot,
Leaking tears.
Plain and model beautiful,
Pressed slacks, no laces in her shoes,
Picking her face to scabs because that's how she feels.
Bound always by the stickiest web of
Musts and expectations,
Never allowing herself to be perfect or imperfect.
She wants to get clean so much
That her hands crack and fester with infection.

---

7. Look him up, you'll be happy you did.

Clay face crumbles into a kabuki smile
As she tears the eyes out of the day
That she ever learned to trust.
Her body is her instrument,
An emotion antenna,
Fingertip sparks curl into a fist ʻ
To punch the next guy who calls her mother a bitch.

    Walking on old souls,
    Dancing on the upturned palms
    Of all she's loved
    And Ever Will.

WHAT I AM TRYING TO DO
> For whom it may make happy.

The red of her face and her breast as she breathes in ecstasy,
The calm of the body that rests easily,
With mind over matter,
Over what matters, matter-of-fact,
With her in the morning of the spring of our children,
Struggling to wake out,
> Open eyes,

Stick my head out the window of Spaceship Earth,
Use my brain made of meat and this fleshy machine to get my genes
From one place to another then back again to where I started
Where the red of his face as he gulpily breathes
Out with the life-scream of all those before him
To shout, "I'm alive, I'm alive, I'm alive."
> There's nothing I need I don't already have 'cause I am a man,
> 'Cause I am a family,
> 'Cause I love a woman and all that she gives me.

The empire I build with thoughts and with words,
The deeds that I have are not written on paper but living within me,
> Without me,

Between me and my God
Who is tellingly feelingly constantly changing me
> No.

I wouldn't exchange all the moneygold wealth
For a second I've spent with my lovely beloveds.

I reserve a dark fist for the mockingly selfish
Blind-as-bat leaders, sucking on blood,
Building their cults on the backs of the trampled
With jury-rigged ignorant fear burning engines
That run on the hatred of that which is different
And when it is taught by schools and by papers,
By parents and siblings, by you and by me,
It's eagerly gulped by beautifully gullible children with their
mouths
Wide open for wisdom,
Getting just dirt,
Taught not to trust in a world full of love.

      That which is different is not instantly foe-ful.
      Teach that to children, see what evolves.

Ambivalence I wanna dance,
I wanna fall into a trance,
A séance to exhume the spirit
All the dead souls who can hear it.
Jump the gap between belief and conviction, emotion behavior,
Linking unlinkables and thinking unthinkables,
Refusing to dwell in the
Escapism guiltism professional confessionalism
Of runaway from selfers

      To examine challengely
      Raise doubt from the dead.

Sitting in the lap of the surf, becoming my abhorrence,
Listen to the rush and recede of anxious currents, which stand on
      Tiptoe
Before diving forward, stretching to reach me with foamy fingers,
      I sit unmoved,
Hoping with my waterheart
For emotion neuro-something to make me move
      In
      Or out.

I survive among my fellow primordial soupsters
'Cause I am a human attempting to live humanly,
Trying to appreciate, trying to relationship,
Verbing my nouns, using my braining to further the cause
      Of tolerant co-existence.

Joy's a balloon that's tied to the moon,
Happy the smile for miles and miles,
Deep is the blue of your mother's eyes,
Warm is the thought
      That I have of you.

STAGE EIGHT: INTEGRITY VS. DESPAIR
(60ISH TO DEATH)

WHY IT HAPPENS

Pour One Out for Those Who Didn't Make It

If you've gotten this far—not in terms of reading this book, but in terms of living a life—congrats. There are way too many humans who, for any number of reasons, have not been able to get through all eight stages. It saddens me to think of the people—family, friends, acquaintances, people I didn't know but heard about, people I never heard about but were great people—who didn't make it. It's important to remember those folks who were robbed of a full life.

To begin, let's pour out a little from our heart to honor those who died too young . . .

This is the most difficult stage for me to write about because I don't benefit from the perspective I had with the other seven stages. I've been through Stages One to Seven. I'm still wading through Stage Eight. So far, it's been a roller coaster of highs and lows, slow stretches, and jarring, dizzying twists —kind of like the previous seven stages. I hope to be around long enough to experience this stage in all its glory and complexity and earn my true OG status (OG is the prototype name for this stage—it stands for Old Guy/Gal/Gangsta/ Geezer/Goat, choose your preferred noun).

Ripening Fruit

If OG has taken care of things and people, learned a little from life's triumphs and disappointments, and generated a few products and ideas here and there, the fruit of the previous seven stages can ripen in them. The result of this ripening is called **integrity.**

It's difficult to fully define integrity, so let me describe someone who has it: An OG with integrity knows what things mean, and they're not afraid to call people out—they have a low threshold for BS; they feel love in their heart, and it's not narcissistic, they love all things human, especially those things which convey some sort of world order and spiritual sense; and they **accept** that their one and only life is something that had to be, no substitutions.

An OG with integrity is aware of the various lifestyles out there which are full of honor and meaning, but is ready to defend the dignity of their own lifestyle against all threats. An OG with integrity knows that their individual lifestyle is the accidental coincidence of their one life cycle with their one segment of history. Further, they understand that their one style of integrity is connected to all human integrity and is supported by their culture and civilization. This integrity seeps deeply into their soul. Death loses its sting.

To exemplify this, I'd like to offer a section from the beautiful eulogy my brother Mark wrote and delivered on the occasion of our mom's death, recounting her last words as he and two of my siblings stood by her bedside:

> . . . *and then Mom very clearly said, "Have I finished my job?" The question spoke volumes about Mom's selfless desire to do the best possible job for everyone —as a patient never wanting to be a burden, as a daughter, as a mother, as a wife. We reassured her that she had indeed done an exemplary job and that if she wanted to move on, she should do that with the affirmation she had completed all of her tasks beautifully. She clearly heard us, and then said a heartfelt and heartbreaking, "Thank you," over and over. Mom's face then softened, her body visibly released its tension, she laid back quietly and said, "We can all go home."*

This is an OG with integrity.

Rage or Accept?

I had worried a lot about my mom up until those final moments. She hated getting old and fought mightily against her body's demise with every ounce of her energy and power. On the one hand, my siblings and I were proud of her raging against the dying of the light[1]; but on the other hand, her

---

1. Read "Do not go gentle into that good night" by Dylan Thomas—it takes

psychologist son (me) worried she wouldn't reach that final stage of grief—acceptance.[2] I worried Mom was being weighed down by an overwhelming fear of death.

If OG has a fear of death at the end of their life, this can mean they don't accept that their one and only life cycle was the one and only life cycle that had to be given their individual and cultural histories. Their regrets overwhelm their accomplishments. These negative feelings can further spiral downward as they recognize that time is too short to start another life and try out alternate roads to integrity. This leads to the negative pole of this crisis continuum—**despair**.

When I was a neophyte psychologist working my rotation through a geriatric care center, I met with a number of bitter, unhappy OGs. I'd diagnose them with varying levels of major depressive disorder, but in my head, all I could think was, *Despair*—sad, disconnected desperation.

Wisdom Is What Wisdom Does

There is no one right way to achieve integrity and its resulting strength, **wisdom**. Line up all the wise older folks and you'll see that there are no surface commonalities. Race, gender, level of wealth, physical or mental attributes, having a great family, having a crappy family—doesn't matter. What does matter is they've all worked openly and honestly through

---

less than a minute and provides the bitterest sweetest view on aging ever.

2. The well-known five stages of grief were developed by Swiss-American psychiatrist Elisabeth Kübler-Ross in 1969. She was a true revolutionary, outlining her theory at a time when no one else wanted to look seriously at death and dying.

the struggles of the previous stages and carry those strengths forward into their later lives.

Each culture has a unique combination of back and forth within these crises that leads to a particular style of integrity, which is further refined by the culture's specific historical place and time. Sometimes having integrity means to be a follower with regard to society's religion or politics or sciences or arts, and sometimes it means accepting the responsibility of leadership.

That said, put all the OGs from across the world in a single room and the ones with wisdom will see each other. Integrity recognizes itself.

The Ninth Stage

When the eight stages were initially charted, Erikson was adamant about not giving any age ranges for the stages because of the variability in the timing of human development. He preferred broader terms such as "infancy," "early childhood," "play age," "school age," "adolescence," "young adulthood," "adulthood," and "old age." But as he grew into his eighties and nineties, he found this time of life brought with it new demands, reevaluations, and daily difficulties. He felt those concerns could only be adequately discussed and confronted by designating a new Ninth Stage of development.

To be clear, Erikson didn't outline an entirely new psychosocial crisis for this stage.[3] He merely observed that no

---

3. The writers of the textbook noted in the references, *Development Through Life: A Psychosocial Approach,* do create a separate psychosocial crisis for "Very Old Age (75 until death)," which they call *Immortality vs. Extinction.*

matter how physically proactive the Very OG (hereafter referred to as the VOG) are, in their eighties and nineties, their body weakens. They can't do what they used to be able to do, and when independence starts to go, so does self-control, self-esteem, and confidence. Recognizing this unavoidable reality of physical, and sometimes mental, deterioration, Erikson shifted the terms of each crisis.

VOG is forced to *mistrust* their own capabilities (Stage One) as hope gives way to frustration in the face of increasing disintegration; they begin to *doubt* their own autonomy (Stage Two); *guilt* raises its ugly head (Stage Three) as purpose and enthusiasm are dulled; there are feelings of *inferiority* (Stage Four) as energy wanes and competence decreases; there's *confusion* about their status and roles (Stage Five) as unwavering lifetime values become less clear in light of new information; they feel more *isolated* (Stage Six) due to their new incapacities; and feelings of *stagnation* may predominate (Stage Seven) because less is demanded of them, leaving them feeling useless.

In Stage Eight, reconceptualized as *Despair vs. Integrity* for those in their eighties and nineties, he notes that the final psychosocial strength to be achieved is wisdom. To be wise, one must be able to see and look, to hear and listen, to touch and feel, and importantly, to remember. How can we be wise if we can't remember where we put our glasses? How can we respond if we can't hear what's being said?

In the struggle between the two poles of this last crisis, as OG becomes VOG, despair can easily win out. During OG's sixties and seventies, there's a lot of retrospective accounting of their life to date. Has life been well-lived? Are there too many regrets? This helps determine the amount of integrity and despair that they experience. But a VOG in their eighties and nineties may no longer have the luxury of this type of retrospection. Loss of physical and mental capacities may take up all their attention as they are forced to focus on just getting through the day intact.

Also, a VOG in their eighties or nineties has likely suffered a lot of loss in their life. Coping with this grief is tough enough, let alone that it signals that death's door is open and not very far away.

Apologies to the VOGs

For those readers in their eighties and nineties, I apologize. That's a lot to take in and it's not very hopeful. I'm getting bummed out writing it.

It's good to remember that much can be accomplished in one's eighties and nineties. Examples abound of vital, productive eighty- and ninety-year-olds: Ben Franklin helped write the US Constitution at eighty-one; Mary Baker Eddy founded the *Christian Science Monitor* at eighty-seven; Hulda Crooks climbed Mount Whitney, the highest mountain in the continental US, at ninety-one; George Burns was still performing at ninety-four; Grandma Moses was still painting at one hundred.

But you don't have to be a genius or a celebrity or a person of extraordinary accomplishment to achieve integrity. Have you been a loving star in your constellation of family and friends? If so, welcome to Integrityville.

And never forget, even if VOG feels like they're psychically drowning, there's a lifeboat that has been there from the very beginning—**basic trust**. Without trust, life is impossible;

with trust, life can be endured. This enduring trust has also bolstered VOG with **hope**. Throughout life, trust may have been dinged, and hope challenged, but they've never left completely. Life without trust and hope is unthinkable. If VOG is filled with the excitement of being able to still take a breath and make a fist, and has a hope for future grace and enlightenment, there is reason to live.

B.P.B.

- People in this stage work toward integrity. An OG with integrity accepts that the life they lived had to be the way it was.
- If an OG's regrets overwhelm their accomplishments, they feel despair.
- There's no one right way to achieve wisdom, but wise people recognize each other.
- As people deal with physical and mental deterioration through their eighties and nineties, working through this crisis becomes challenging and difficult.
- Trust and hope, which were (hopefully) learned in Stage One, help OG and VOG find reasons to live.

WHAT TO DO

Reinvention

Some cultures, philosophers, and theorists have taken a broader view than Erikson and divided the life cycle into three stages. The first stage, from birth to about age thirty, is a time of *learning*, where a person builds skills and knowledge so that they'll be able to engage in the roles of adulthood. The second stage, between thirty and sixty, is a period of *enactment,* where a person's life is shaped by their work, family, and community expectations.

The final stage, between sixty and ninety, can be seen as a period of *reinvention.* The demands of work and family slowly fall away and there is an opportunity to invent a new life structure. Though there may be significant adversity during this stage, it can also be a time of great joy.

As someone in this stage, the idea of reinvention is inspiring. As I passed my sixtieth birthday and retired, I was hit with a tsunami of emotion, most of it shitty. The kids were grown with families of their own; I had undervalued the meaningfulness that my work had brought me; I struggled to write anything, because who the hell wants to hear what an old guy has to say?

So I embraced (or I'm trying to embrace) this idea of reinvention, and it helps. At least it's helped me write this (which I've been planning to do since I was thirty but for some reason never got around to it).

I was so excited about this idea that I wanted to proselytize it to others in a similar situation. I discussed it with my siblings and my mom on a COVID-era Zoom call—0–30 learning, 30–60 enactment, 60–90 reinvention—and my mom, who was ninety-two at the time, ever spunky, said, "What about *me*?" Touché, Mom.

Indulge Your Dependencies

Reconciling generativity and stagnation can lead to grand-generativity in the OG. No longer does OG have direct responsibility for maintaining the world, but they still have roles—aging parent, grandparent, old friend, mentor—which provide social opportunities to experience grand-generativity in relationships with people of all ages. OG needs to take those opportunities.

As OG becomes VOG, it becomes more of a two-way street. They care for others but they're also challenged to accept care from others. It's all part of the generational cycle. Good OGs and VOGs enhance feelings of generativity in their younger caregivers.

This is best exemplified by a phrase offered up by Morrie Schwartz, the protagonist in the book *Tuesdays with Morrie* by Mitch Albom.[4] In recounting his physical decline, Morrie employed the "Wipe your own ass" test—was he still able to do this simple function? When not able to perform that task for himself, Morrie said you must, "Indulge your dependencies," which basically means, don't be a martyr. Let other people help you when you need help. Simple and profound advice I found myself sharing with many clients in my practice, regardless of their age.

---

4. Morrie was an incredibly insightful and giving man who was able to explicate many important ideas about death as he himself was dying. I'd show Morrie's interview with *Nightline's* Ted Koppel when I taught end-of-life issues to college students.

Playless Childhood

In keeping with Erikson's psycho*social* approach, there are things that a society can do to make it better for VOGs.

Long-lived elders of ancient times were applauded and revered. This too often is not the case in modern society's youth-obsessed culture. VOGs are ignored or worse, disrespected. Help may be offered, but often VOG is left feeling useless and infantilized. When I was a young psychologist working with this population, my supervisor[5] observed me interacting on the unit, then brought me back to his office and told me, "Martino, don't be helpful." Confused at first because I was a young idiot, eventually I realized—don't do for VOG what they can do for themself.

We want VOG to have a second childhood, but the one we give them seems totally playless. Homes for VOGs are planned like big hotels to serve all their obvious needs, and to be clear, much good, commendable work is done at such places, but there's a big if—*if* the VOG has the dough to afford it.

The other problem with such facilities is that they tend to segregate the VOGs from the rest of the world. Social support is the backbone of healthy aging, and even though VOG has their needs taken care of, there is still an "us" and "them" division that permeates such facilities.

How can young people learn from VOG if they don't live near each other? If you have the good fortune of living in close contact with friends or relatives in their nineties, you'll be able to more fully share their experience of what life becomes in the Ninth Stage.

---

5. The great Dr. Paul Fedirka—if you don't know him, your loss.

How about this for an idea: Every city builds good, well-guarded parks available to all, and in the middle of each park would be a residence for elders. The elders would be able to take short walks or rides in wheelchairs within the park with their relatives and friends, who could speak to them, hear their stories, and learn from their wisdom.

Too unrealistic? It would take personal and political commitment unclouded by the fears and anxieties most folks have about growing old and dying. But it'd be worth it.

When I'm in a wheelchair, roll me to a park and let me watch kids play. That would make me happy.

Gerotranscendence

If elders can deal with all the shit that's thrown their way later in life, they may be on the path to **gerotranscendence**—they focus less on the physical stuff in their lives, and more on the stuff they can't see, like cosmic and spiritual stuff. VOGs on this path tend to be happier. It's the final stage in a natural process toward maturation and wisdom.

As time winnows down to the present and space decreases to what physical limitations dictate, a gerotranscendent VOG recognizes they are connected to so many other people; they feel a peacefulness about the world and their place in it; and they accept that death is the way of all living things.

For a gerotranscendent VOG, the race and competition are over. They may withdraw, but it's consciously chosen. They may continue to be involved despite the disengagement, which Erikson called, "Deeply involved disinvolvement."

Unfortunately, some VOGs are forced into withdrawal due to physical limitation or societal mores. Too often VOGs are placed where they are rarely seen or heard. Gerotranscendence in the face of imposed withdrawal is less likely, but not impossible.

Act Your Age

The normal societal model for old age has been to encourage letting go, but not to seek a new life or role, not to reinvent. We praise VOG for striving to look or act young. This is, in a word, bullshit. Trying to be younger is playacting. It stifles normal development.

The trick is to confront aging without delusion. Discover the freedom to go beyond the limits imposed by the world— *This is how I look. This is who I am. I will not apologize for the years I have lived.* Keep going, keep doing things for as long as you can—play; be open to joy; sing a song; join a writer's group.

The body may be old and imperfect but there is still and always will be so much beauty in this world, or as Keats said:

Beauty is truth, truth beauty—that is all
Ye know on earth, and all ye need to know.[6]

The Rocky Path

Remember those folks we honored at the top of this chapter, the ones who didn't make it? In their memory we say: To grow old is a great privilege. To live a long life and to be able to relive it in retrospect? What a blessing.

But growing old is not for cowards. The Ninth Stage is the

---

6. From *Ode on a Grecian Urn* by John Keats.

final Hero's Journey in a lifetime of Hero's Journeys. Gotta face that fear of death. Gotta take a trusting (that word again!) leap into the greatest of unknowns. Gotta be humble. Gotta be *really* humble. Gotta finish this life to create a legacy to add to the world. Gotta get into infinity.

This final journey tends to be on a narrow, steep hill littered with rocks and trash. So what to do? Take a step, and another, and another. With each step you get higher, and the vistas get more and more rewarding. And since it can be a tricky path, you're gonna need to lighten your load and unburden yourself.

It takes a lifetime of experience to successfully navigate this final path. It's easy to blame the terrain, the wind, the too-bright light if you find yourself backsliding. So take a rest. Have a snack. There's no time for self-pity or weakening of purpose. Set your face to the rising sun, watch out for loose gravel, try to maintain your pace. Sometimes you'll want to keep going; sometimes you'll want to stop. That's good. All along it's been about that back and forth, that yin and yang, that interpersonal wrestling match. Every step is a challenge, a test. That tension is at the root of your success.

B.P.B.[7]

- Learn things the first thirty years, do things the next thirty years, then dedicate the next thirty years or so to reinventing yourself.

---

7. I bet you forgot what "B.P.B." stands for.

- Don't be a martyr during this stage—let other people help you when you need help.
- If you're helping a VOG, don't do things for them they can do for themself.
- VOGs who work toward gerotranscendence— change their focus from material things to spirituality and connection—tend to be happier.
- VOGs who act their age will negotiate the final path with more peace and insight.

Thanks Mom

This may be cliché, but I'd like to end by going to the dictionary. *Webster's* defines **trust** as, "The assured reliance on another's **integrity**." Erikson himself said, "Healthy children will not fear life if their elders have integrity enough not to fear death."

At the end, my mom didn't fear death, which makes me fear life a lot less. So to Mom and to all the courageous elders who have faced their final days with grace and dignity, I'd like to repeat what she said as she left this world: "Thank you thank you thank you thank you thank you thank you thank you thank you thank you thank you . . ."

Now go home . . . but read one more poem before you go.

THE OWL AND THE PUSSYCAT . . . AND MORE

By Edward Lear (I-III) and me (IV-VI)

I

The Owl and the Pussycat went to sea
In a beautiful pea-green boat.
They took some honey, and plenty of money,
Wrapped up in a five-pound note.
The Owl looked up to the stars above,
And sang to a small guitar,
"O lovely Pussy, O Pussy, my love,
What a beautiful Pussy you are,
You are,
You are!
What a beautiful Pussy you are!"

II

Pussy said to the Owl, "You elegant fowl!
How charmingly sweet you sing!
Oh! Let us be married; too long we have tarried.
But what shall we do for a ring?"
They sailed away, for a year and a day,
To the land where the bong tree grows.
And there in the wood a Piggywig stood,
With a ring at the end of his nose,
His nose,
His nose,
With a ring at the end of his nose.

III

"Dear Pig, are you willing to sell for one shilling
Your ring?" Said the Piggy, "I will."
So they took it away, and were married next day
By the Turkey who lives on the hill.
They dined on mince and slices of quince,
Which they ate with a runcible spoon.
And hand in hand, on the edge of the sand
They danced by the light of the moon,
The moon,
The moon,
They danced by the light of the moon.

IV

The Owl and the Pussycat went to sleep
After dancing the night away.
They dreamed of hearts, and raspberry tarts,
Until the first light of day.
Owl awoke to Pussy's soft stroke,
And gazed at her twinkling eyes,
"O lovely Pussy, O Pussy, my love,
I'll love you until I may die,
May die,
May die,
I'll love you until I may die."

V

Pussy then said from her dry sandy bed,
"Our love is as big as the sea!
Oh Owl, let us do, have a child or two,
And hold them until they go free."
Owl wholly agreed that with egg and some seed,
A wonderful baby would grow,
And soon there was born, one fine sunny morn,
A boy who was smiling, "Hello,
Hello,
Hello,"
A boy who was smiling, "Hello."

VI

The boy had a brother he loved like no other,
The family grew with such ease.
They packed all their troubles on billowous bubbles,
And let them go free in the breeze.
The brothers then rowed, as their parents grew old
And waved from their place on the shore,
Out into the sea, where the fishes run free;
They watched till they could see no more,
No more,
No more,
They watched till they could see no more.

OPPORTUNITY TO CONNECT

Invite Dr. Dave to your event, book club, or podcast!

Looking to add wisdom, wit, and a touch of seasoned insight to your event, book club, or podcast? Dr. Dave brings decades of experience as a psychologist, educator, guest expert, invited speaker, father, and a writer with a sharp sense of humor. He's well-versed in what it takes to raise good humans and be a decent one yourself—and he's ready to share that knowledge with warmth, candor, and just the right amount of irreverence.

If you've read *Life in Eight Stages: What to Know to Raise and Be a Human*—or if you're about to—Dr. Dave will join your gathering, in person or virtually, to ~~shamelessly plug his book~~ offer thoughtful insights, lively discussion, and practical takeaways you won't forget. Minimal care and feeding required.

To schedule an event: email: dr.martino2020@gmail.com, or visit his website: davidmartinophd.com.

Before you go…

Please consider leaving an honest review on Amazon or Goodreads, or if you didn't like the book, a less-than-honest review will suffice. Reviews help spread the word and are greatly appreciated by the author.

REFERENCES
PEOPLE SMARTER THAN ME

Erikson, Erik H. 1950. *Childhood and Society*. W. W. Norton & Company, Inc.

Erikson, Erik H. and Schlien, S (ed.). 1987. *A Way of Looking at Things: Selected papers from 1930 to 1980*. W. W. Norton & Company.

Erikson, Joan M. 1997. *The Life Cycle Completed: Extended Version*. W.W. Norton & Company, Inc.

Freud, Sigmund. 1927. *So's Yo Mama: An Analysis of Yo Mama Jokes and Why She So Fat*. Oxford Community College Press.

Fuller, R. Buckminster. 1970. *I Seem To Be A Verb*. Bantam Books.

Jung, Carl. 1961. *The Jung and The Restless: The Hopes and Fears of Genoa City*. Jack & Katherine & Company.

Kübler-Ross, Elisabeth. 1969. *On Death and Dying*. Macmillan Publishers.

Lear, Edward. 1967. *Edward Lear's Nonsense Books*. Grosset & Dunlap, Inc.

Newman, B. M. and Newman, P. R. 2006. *Development Through Life: A Psychosocial Approach* (I taught out of the 9th edition but there's probably editions after that). Thomson Wadsworth.

Ringo, Doctor. 1961. *Some of These References Are Real and Some Are Not: Figure Out Which Is Which*. Faux Soup Publications.

Sternberg, R. J. and Barnes, M. L. (eds.). 1988. *The Psychology of Love*. Yale University Press.

ABOUT THE AUTHOR

David Martino has a Ph.D. in clinical-developmental psychology and has worked as a clinical psychologist, teacher, husband and dad (the last two jobs by far the most difficult and rewarding). He has been an invited pundit and guest expert in newspapers and on radio and television. He has published children's books, song lyrics, and an article in the sadly-defunct *Journal of Polymorphous Perversity.* Two of his original full-length plays and some of his shorter theater pieces have been produced and performed in regional theaters. For over twenty years he has written sketch comedy and monologues for an ongoing live variety show, which he describes as, "Like SNL, but funnier." Currently he's working on writing his own obituary. If you see him on the bike trails of Fort Collins, CO (his natural habitat), offer him some water and a snack.

www.ingramcontent.com/pod-product-compliance
Lightning Source LLC
Chambersburg PA
CBHW030841090426
42737CB00009B/1061